CW00959634

Wuthering Heights

A play

April De Angelis
From the novel by Emily Brontë

Samuel French — London
www.samuelfrench-london.co.uk

WUTHERING HEIGHTS

First produced in association with the Touring Consortium at the Birmingham Repertory Theatre in October 2008 with the following cast:

Heathcliff	Antony Byrne
Cathy/Young Cathy	Amanda Ryan
Nelly Dean	Susannah York
Mr Lockwood	Simon Coates
Hindley/Hareton	Edmund Kingsley
Joseph/Old Mr Linton	David Whitworth
Edgar/Linton	Toby Dantzic
Frances/Mary	Victoria Yeates
Isabella/Zillah	Emma Noakes
Jabes Branderham/Servant/Lad	Martin Allanson

Directed by Indhu Rubasingham

CHARACTERS

Heathcliff
Cathy
Edgar Linton
Young Cathy, daughter of Cathy
Nelly Dean, servant
Mr Lockwood, tenant of Thrushcross Grange
Hindley, Cathy's elder brother
Hareton, Hindley's son
Joseph, servant
Mr Linton, Edgar and Isabella's father
Frances, Hindley's wife
Mary, young servant
Isabella Linton, Edgar's younger sister
Zillah, servant
Jabes Branderham, a reverend
Servant
Lad
Band of Musicians

SYNOPSIS OF SCENES

The action of the play spans several years.
Time — early Victorian

AUTHOR'S NOTE

I had intended this piece as a kind of rough theatre — where actors did much of the moving furniture, using simple props, reacting to "invisible" dogs, etc. The idea was to keep the piece as fluid as possible so it had a kind of story telling aesthetic. Mr Lockwood could be seated at the side of the stage apart from the action as he is a kind of voyeur, or watcher, but able to come into the action and observe if the production desired it.

Other plays by April De Angelis
published by Samuel French Ltd

Playhouse Creatures

ACT I
Scene 1

Wuthering Heights. Evening

Both the interior and exterior of the house can be seen. Inside there is a kitchen with a table and chairs, a fireplace, a bookshelf, cupboards and a tray of tea things

Lockwood appears outside the house. He definitely has something of the tourist about him. He addresses the audience as if his concerns are everybody's

Lockwood This is certainly a beautiful country. In all England, I do not think I could have fixed on a situation so completely removed from the stir of society. Wuthering Heights. (*Looking it up in his guide book*) "Wuthering being a significant provincial adjective, descriptive of the atmospheric tumult to which its station is exposed in stormy weather. Happily, the architect had the foresight to build the house strong; the narrow windows deeply set into the wall, the corners defended with large jutting stones, all set about with gaunt thorns and stunted firs — a perfect misanthropist's heaven!"
Women are fascinating creatures but I have removed myself from their presence as a kindness to them. I must never break another heart.

He knocks on the door. There is the sound of dogs barking

(*Calling*) Hello there! I've come to call upon Mr Heathcliff. I'm Mr Lockwood, his new tenant.

There is more barking

Joseph, an old servant, looks through a window and opens it

Joseph (*shouting*) T'maister's dahn i't'fowld. Goa rahnd by th'end ut'laith if yah went tuh spake tull him.

Joseph bangs the window shut

There is more barking. Lockwood knocks again

Lockwood Open the door, will you?

Joseph opens the window

Joseph There's nobbut t'missis and shoo'll not open't an ye mak yer flaysome dins 'til neeght.
Lockwood Pardon?
Joseph There's nobbut t'missis!
Lockwood Can't you tell her who I am?
Joseph Nor-ne me! Aw'll hae noa hend w'it.

Joseph slams the window shut

The wind howls and snow begins to fall

Hareton enters, carrying a pitchfork

Lockwood (*to Hareton*) Sir, I don't seem to be able to make myself understood. I'm Mr Heathcliff's new tenant at the Thrushcross Grange. I wish to see him. (*He pauses*) It's snowing.
Hareton Better come in.
Lockwood At last I am to be formally received.

Hareton and Lockwood enter the house. Hareton takes off his coat.

They join Joseph and Young Cathy, who is sitting at the table. No one takes any notice of Lockwood

(*Bowing to Young Cathy*) Mr Lockwood, at your service.

Young Cathy does nothing. Lockwood shakes the snow off himself

Rough weather, I'm afraid, Mrs Heathcliff. The floor must bear the consequence. I had hard work to make your servants hear me.
Young Cathy Mrs Heathcliff!

Young Cathy jumps up in disgust and moves away. She gets a tray of tea things and places it on the table

Hareton Sit down. He'll be in soon.

A chair is placed for Lockwood. He sits. The dog snarls

Juno, behave!

Lockwood A beautiful animal, ma'am.

Lockwood pets Juno uncertainly. Juno snaps at him

Young Cathy She's not mine.

Lockwood stares at Young Cathy. She turns to reach for a book on the shelf. Lockwood sees her difficulty and gets up to help her

Lockwood Let me?
Young Cathy I don't want your help. I can get it for myself.

Lockwood oogles her. Young Cathy stretches higher

Lockwood I would hate to see your delicate form take a tumble.
Young Cathy (*getting the book*) Were you asked to tea?
Lockwood You should be the one to ask me.
Young Cathy Did I ask you?
Lockwood No.
Joseph (*to Young Cathy*) Aw woonder hagh yah can fashion to stand thear i'idleness. Yah'll never mend yer ill ways; bud goa raight tub t'divil like yer mother afore ye!
Young Cathy Scandalous old hypocrite! Aren't you afraid of being carried off by the devil when you mention his name? I'll ask him to do it as a special favour. I've progressed in the black arts! (*She waves the book at Joseph*)
Joseph Oh, wicked, wicked! May the Lord deliver us from evil!

The wind blows the front door open. Healthcliff stands in the doorway as snow blows in and dogs howl

The maister!
Lockwood Mr Heathcliff. I am your new tenant at the Grange, come according to promise.
Heathcliff I wonder you should select the thick of a snowstorm to ramble about in? People familiar with these moors often miss their roads on such evenings. (*To Young Cathy*) Are you going to make th'tea?
Young Cathy Is he to have any?
Heathcliff Get it ready, will you? (*To Lockwood*) Sit down.

Lockwood draws up around the table. Young Cathy pours the tea. There is an awkward pause

Lockwood Many could not imagine the existence of happiness in a life of such complete exile from the world as you spend, Mr Heathcliff. Yet I'll venture to say that surrounded by your family and with your amiable lady as the presiding genius over your home and hearth—

Heathcliff (*bashing his fist down on the table*) My amiable lady! Where is she?

Lockwood Mrs Heathcliff — your wife, I mean ——

Heathcliff My wife is dead. She is my daughter-in-law.

Lockwood Ah, certainly, I see now. (*To Hareton*) This young gentleman is the favoured possessor of the beneficent fairy.

Hareton spits out his tea

Heathcliff Unhappy in your conjectures, sir, we neither of us have the privilege of owning your good fairy. Her mate is dead. She is my daughter-in-law, therefore, she must have married my son.

Lockwood And this young man is ...

Heathcliff Not my son.

Hareton My name is Hareton Earnshaw and I'd counsel you to respect it.

Lockwood Well, this has been delightful. I think I must get home now. The roads will be buried. I'll scarcely distinguish a foot in advance. I'll need a guide. Could you spare me one?

Heathcliff No.

Lockwood Then I must trust to my own sagacity.

Heathcliff You'll be lost, then. Hareton, drive the dozen sheep into the barn porch.

Joseph exits

Hareton gets up and puts on his coat

Lockwood How must I do?

Heathcliff shrugs. Young Cathy goes to warm herself by the fire

Mrs Heathcliff, you must excuse me for troubling you. With that face you must be good-hearted. Do point out some landmarks by which I may know my way home. I have no more idea how to get there than you would have to get to London.

Young Cathy Take the road you came.

Lockwood If you hear of me dead in a bog, won't your conscience whisper to you that it was your fault?

Young Cathy How so? I cannot escort you. They don't let me get to the end of the garden wall.

Joseph enters, carrying a lantern

Heathcliff I hope it will be a lesson to you to make no more rash journeys! You must share a bed with Hareton or Joseph. I don't keep accommodations for visitors.

Lockwood I can sleep here on this chair.

Heathcliff No. You'll not have the range of the place while I'm off guard.

Lockwood Then, sir, I will make my own way.

Hareton I'll go with him as far as the park.

Heathcliff You'll go with him to hell. Who's to see to the horses?

Young Cathy A man's life is of more consequence than one night's neglect of the horses.

Hareton You be quiet. You don't command me.

Young Cathy No. Who could command a block of wood? (*To Heathcliff*) I hope Mr Lockwood dies and his ghost haunts you, Mr Heathcliff, and you never get another tenant 'til the Grange is a ruin!

Young Cathy runs out

Joseph Harken, harken shoo's cursing on 'em!

Lockwood I bid you goodnight. (*He tries to grab the lantern from Joseph*)

Joseph Maister, he's staling t'lantern, maister!

The dogs bark

Hey Gnasher. Hey Wolf — hold him, hold him.

The dogs grapple Lockwood to the ground. Heathcliff and Hareton laugh

Zillah, a servant, runs in

Zillah Are we going to murder folk on our very doorstones? Look at t'poor lad. He's fair choking. I'll cure that. (*She throws a bucket of cold water on Lockwood*) There now. That's better.

The dogs disperse

Heathcliff Not bitten, are you?

Lockwood A herd of possessed swine could have no worse spirits in them than those animals of yours, sir.

Heathcliff They won't meddle with persons who touch nothing. They do right to be vigilant. (*To Zillah*) Show him to bed.

Heathcliff, Joseph and Hareton exit

SCENE 2

A moment later

Zillah and Lockwood traverse the house towards a bedroom, where there is a bed next to a window with shutters, and a bookshelf. Zillah carries a candle

Zillah Make no noise. Master has an odd notion of the chamber I'll put you in.

Lockwood For what reason?

Zillah I don't know. So many queer goings-on. (*She hands him the candle*) Goodnight.

Zillah exits

Lockwood Zillah?

He sits on the bed and as he brings the candle to the window writing appears on it

(*Reading*) "Catherine Earnshaw, Catherine Heathcliff, Catherine Linton." (*He finds a book; reading*) "Seventy sins times seven; a pious discourse delivered by the Reverend Jabes Branderham in the chapel of Gimmerden Sough." Lively bedtime reading! (*He looks in the book then turns it on its side to read in the margin and discerns by the light of his candle*) What's written here in the margins? Stinking old book. (*Reading*) "Heathcliff and I took the dingy volume by the scroop and hurled it into the dog kennel. Poor Heathcliff. Hindley calls him a vagabond and says we must not play together and threatens to turn him out if we break his orders …"

Lockwood yawns and falls asleep, dropping the book. We see his dream as he dreams it

A Crowd of people including Branderham enter the room, carrying staves. They are led by Joseph. The Crowd jostle and sway

Joseph To the chapel!

Crowd To hear Jabes Branderham preach!

Branderham (*booming*) There'll be four hundred and ninety parts to the sermon.

Crowd Four hundred and ninety parts!

Lockwood (*moaning*) Four hundred and ninety parts!

The Crowd cheer and beat their staves on the ground

Branderham Part the first!

Crowd Part the first.

The Crowd beat their staves. Lockwood groans, writhes and tries to block out the sound

Branderham What follows is an unpardonable sin beyond the ordinary scale of human wrongs. Your poor, sinful bodies stretched out on hot gridirons in the nethermost fiery pit of hell. Hell is real, not all humans are saved!

Lockwood Sir! I have endured too much! (*To the Crowd*) Fellow martyrs, have at him and crush him to atoms!

Branderham One of us has committed the unpardonable sin!

Crowd He must be publicly exposed! Excommunicated.

Branderham (*pointing to Lockwood*) Thou art the man! Brethren, execute upon him the judgment written!

The Crowd turn on Lockwood, banging their staves on the ground

Lockwood (*crying out*) No! (*He wakes up with a gasp*)

The Crowd, Branderham and Joseph disappear

A tree branch taps against the window and the wind is wuthering. Lockwood tries to sleep. The tapping is insistent. Exasperated, he gets up to open the window

As he reaches, a white hand reaches in through the window and grasps his. We see Cathy, as a child, at the window

Cathy Let me in. Let me in.

Lockwood Who are you?

Cathy Catherine Linton. I'm come home. I'd lost my way on the moor.

Lockwood Let me go.
Cathy Let me in.
Lockwood No.

Cathy rubs her hand on the broken pane of glass. She cries out as blood runs

Cathy Ah! Let me in. I beg you.
Lockwood How can I? Let me go and I'll let you in.

Cathy lets go

Be gone. I'll never let you in, not if you beg for twenty years. (*He struggles to close the window*)
Cathy It is twenty years. Twenty years I've been wandering for. Twenty years!

Lockwood lets out a chilling yell, pushes Cathy out and slams the window shutters closed

Cathy goes. Heathcliff enters

Heathcliff Who's there?
Lockwood It is only your guest, sir. I had the misfortune to scream in my sleep, owing to a frightful nightmare.
Heathcliff God confound you, Mr Lockwood. Who showed you to this room?
Lockwood Your servant, Zillah.
Heathcliff I'll turn her out!
Lockwood (*dressing rapidly*) I would. She richly deserves it. I suppose she wanted to get another proof that this place was haunted at my expense. Well, it is swarming with ghosts and goblins.
Heathcliff What?
Lockwood If the little fiend had got in at the window she would probably have strangled me. Catherine Linton or Earnshaw or however she was called — wicked little soul. She told me she had been walking the earth these twenty years; a just punishment for mortal transgressions I've no doubt!
Heathcliff How dare you ... under my roof! Mr Lockwood, you may go to my room. You'll only be in the way downstairs and your childish outcry has sent sleep to the devil for me.
Lockwood And for me, too. I'll walk in the yard 'til daylight and then I'll be off. And you need not dread a repetition of my company. I am now quite cured of seeking pleasure in society. Good-day.

Lockwood exits

Heathcliff (*wrenching open the window and shutters; crying*) Come in! Come in, Cathy, do come. Oh do, once more my heart's darling. Hear me this time, Catherine, at last!

The Lights fade to Black-out

SCENE 3

Outside Thrushcross Grange. The next day

Lockwood sits with a blanket over him. He sneezes into a handkerchief

Nelly Dean, a servant, enters with some breakfast for Lockwood

Nelly Mr Heathcliff walked you across the moors, did he?
Lockwood Yes.
Nelly He left you here at the entrance to the Grange?
Lockwood Yes.
Nelly And then you got lost amongst the trees and buried up to your neck in snow?
Lockwood Yes. (*He sneezes*)
Nelly (*arranging Lockwood's blanket*) I won't disturb you, Mr Lockwood. I know you've forsworn all company.
Lockwood Thank you. That's very sensitive.

Nelly goes to exit

Mrs Dean?
Nelly Yes.
Lockwood I'm bored stiff. I've put up a valiant struggle with solitude all day. Not spoken to a soul. You couldn't stay and gossip to me, could you?
Nelly Can anything I say be of interest to you? I thought you cared nothing for human affairs?
Lockwood Tell me everything. I've a fancy to hear about the history of Mr Heathcliff and that very pretty girl widow.
Nelly Young Cathy?
Lockwood Is she a native? More likely an exotic. The most exquisite little face I've ever seen, a delicate neck, admirable form and the most delicious —
Nelly Yes. Before I became housekeeper here at the Grange I was almost always at Wuthering Heights. One fine summer morning, many years

ago, Mr Earnshaw, the old master, told his family he was going to Liverpool. He asked his children, Cathy and Hindley ——

Cathy and Hindley enter, as children

— what they wanted for a present. Hindley wished for a ——

Nelly   } (*together*) Fiddle.
Hindley

Nelly And Cathy, that's the mother of young Cathy ——
Lockwood That aroused my ——
Nelly Attention. She chose ——

Nelly   } (*together*) A whip.
Cathy

Nelly He promised me a pocketful of apples and pears. But when he came back he had none of these. He opens up his greatcoat and there it was; a dirty, ragged, black-haired child. It spoke some gibberish nobody could understand. "You must take it as a gift of God," he says, "though it's as dark almost as it came from the devil." Mrs Earnshaw was ready to fling it out of doors. "Am I to bring up a gypsy brat when I've my own bairns to feed and fend for?" she cries. "I found it starving, as good as dumb in the streets of Liverpool!" says Mr Earnshaw. "I thought it better to take it home. We'll call him Heathcliff after our son that died."

Lockwood A foundling!
Nelly The ruination of us!

Heathcliff enters, as a child

Hindley Have you my fiddle, Father?
Cathy And my whip?
Nelly "Broken, children," says Mr Earnshaw.

Hindley and Cathy stare at Heathcliff

Nelly Hindley hated him. Maybe because Old Mr Earnshaw had taken such a shine to him.

Hindley runs at him and strikes Heathcliff a blow

Hindley Stinking Gypsy.

Heathcliff doesn't flinch

Nelly Heathcliff would stand Hindley's blows without shedding a tear.

Hindley I'll make you cry like a girl.

Hindley hits Heathcliff again, and again Heathcliff doesn't flinch or retaliate. He stands his ground. This spooks Hindley

Cathy Leave him. You'll not make him cry.
Hindley (*running off*) He can't make me cry either.

Hindley exits

Cathy stares at Heathcliff. They move towards each other in mutual fascination

Nelly Cathy and Heathcliff grew very thick.
Lockwood What did they do?
Nelly Played the usual children's games.
Cathy Heathcliff! Let's raise the dead in the churchyard!

Cathy and Heathcliff stand on imaginary graves and raise their hands to the sky

Rise up sinners.
Cathy
Heathcliff } (*together*) Speak to us your secrets from beyond the grave!

Joseph enters and chases Cathy and Heathcliff

Joseph Heathens! Yah'll never mend yer ill ways; bud goa raight tub t'divil.

Cathy and Heathcliff avoid being caught by Joseph. They laugh and tease him, mocking him by repeating what he says and hiding

Nelly Her spirits were always at high watermark — her tongue always going — singing, laughing, plaguing everybody who would not do the same. A wild, wick-slip, she was much too fond of Heathcliff.

Joseph and others catch Cathy and Heathcliff

The greatest punishment we could invent was to keep her separate from him.
Cathy Heathcliff! It's my fault. I put him up to it.
Heathcliff Cathy! Don't say so. It was me that did it.

They are separated. Heathcliff receives blows

Nelly When the master and mistress died ——
Lockwood They died?
Nelly Be warned, Mr Lockwood, people have a habit of dying in this
tale.

Cathy and Heathcliff join hands and exit

(*She watches them go*) The two little souls comforted each other. They
pictured heaven so beautifully, I could not help wishing we were all
there safe together.
Lockwood I'm looking forward to heaven myself, Mrs Dean, but not
quite yet.
Nelly Hindley was master now. He returned for the funeral, changed
after three years absence, and what amazed us and set the neighbours
gossiping right and left — he brought a wife.

The Lights fade to Black-out

SCENE 4

Wuthering Heights

*Hindley enters with Frances, who rushes in ahead of him. She exclaims
at any object she chances upon*

*Nelly can move between the scene and Lockwood has the freedom of a
narrator*

Frances Oh, how lovely! The floor! The fireplace! The cupboard! The
dog kennel! (*She laughs a little hysterically*)
Nelly Every object delighted her.

Heathcliff and Cathy enter, wearing black

Frances screams and retreats

Except the young people.
Frances They're wearing black!
Nelly They're in mourning, ma'am. Their father's dead.
Frances Can't they wear another colour?
Nelly Black is traditional.

Frances It frightens me. I'm terribly scared of dying, Nelly.

Hindley You and Joseph must quarter yourselves in the back kitchen, Nelly, and leave the house for Frances and myself. Things will be done differently from now on.

Frances I shall be happy to have a new brother and sister! Even if they do wear *that* colour.

Hindley You shall be happy in a sister only. (*Indicating Heathcliff*) He is a servant. There's plenty of work in the fields. Lads work hard out there, why shouldn't he? There's to be no more scrounging off us and no more lessons from the curate, either.

Cathy Father would not like that, Hindley. Heathcliff should be cared for as we are.

Hindley I am master now, Cathy, and to be obeyed in all things. He's to eat in the outhouse, not with us.

Cathy That's cruel banishment.

Hindley He should be grateful for every mouthful. (*Indicating to leave*) Frances.

Hindley and Frances exit

Heathcliff How will you like me as a servant, Cathy?

Cathy I'll teach you what I'm taught, Heathcliff. You'll not get behind me. And when you're working in the fields I'll come and play there with you. And on Sundays we'll run away to the moors and stay all day with no one to tell us what to do. We'll not go to chapel. They can flog us 'til their arms ache. Deny us supper. We'll laugh at our punishments. (*Holding out her hand to Heathcliff*) Let's run away to the moors.

Nelly Many a time I've cried to myself to watch them growing more reckless daily yet not daring to speak for fear of losing the small power I still retained over the unfriended creatures.

Cathy No one cares for us but us.

Cathy pulls Heathcliff away and off they run

The Lights fade to Black-out

SCENE 5

The same. There is wind, rain and darkness. Joseph and Hindley are inside

Nelly enters with a lantern

Nelly (*calling*) Cathy! Heathcliff!

Hindley Have they not been discovered?

Nelly We've searched high and low. It's a wicked night.

Hindley Bolt the doors against them. On pain of dismissal, nobody let them in this night.

Joseph goes to bolt the doors

Nelly gets a candle and looks out of a window. She sees a lantern glimmering in the dark and hurries out

Nelly (*whispering*) Who's there?

Heathcliff emerges

Heathcliff? Shh. Don't let Hindley hear you. Where is Miss Catherine? No accident, I hope?

Heathcliff She's at the Grange. I have been there too but they had not the manners to ask me to stay.

Nelly Well, you will catch it. What in the world led you wandering to the Grange?

Heathcliff Let me out of my wet clothes.

They enter the house. Heathcliff takes off his wet shirt and rubs himself dry with it

Cathy and I escaped. We ran from the top of the Heights to the Grange without stopping, Catherine completely beaten in the race because she was barefoot. You'll have to seek for her shoes in the bog tomorrow. We thought we would just go and see how the Linton children passed their Sundays.

Nelly They are good children, no doubt, and do not deserve the punishments you get.

Heathcliff We planted ourselves on a flowerpot under the drawing-room window. We clung to the ledge. What did we see?

In tableau, Isabella and Edgar Linton can be seen. Cathy stands before a mimed window and peeps in

Heathcliff moves into the frame of the story, as he narrates and talks to Nelly

Cathy A splendid place, carpeted with crimson.

Heathcliff And crimson-covered chairs and tables.

Cathy From the ceiling, a shower of glass drops hanging from silver chains!

Heathcliff Edgar and his sister had it entirely to themselves. We should have thought ourselves in heaven. What were your good children doing? Isabella was shrieking as if witches were running red hot needles into her eyes.

Cathy Edgar stood weeping.

Heathcliff A little dog sat by them which they'd nearly pulled apart between them.

Cathy The idiots!

Heathcliff That was their pleasure; to quarrel who should hold a heap of warm hair. When would you catch me wishing to have what Catherine wanted or find us seeking entertainment in yelling and sobbing and rolling on the ground?

Nelly Hush now, hush. Tell me how Catherine is left behind.

Cathy laughs

Heathcliff The Lintons heard us. They shot like arrows to the door.

The Linton children do so, coming outside of the picture frame

Edgar ⎱ (*together*) Oh Papa come. Papa, Papa!
Isabella ⎰

Heathcliff "Papa! Papa!" We made frightful noises to terrify them still more.

Heathcliff and Cathy howl like animals. Heathcliff joins the scene fully

Edgar ⎱ (*together*) Papa!
Isabella ⎰

Mr Linton runs on, followed by a Servant with a bulldog

Servant At 'em, Skulker!
Heathcliff Flee, Cathy!

The dog pounces on Cathy

Cathy Run, Heathcliff, run! They have let the bulldog loose and he holds me.

Heathcliff I heard his abominable snorting, Nelly, but she did not yell out. She would have scorned to do it if she had been spitted on the horns of a mad cow.

Cathy twists and turns in agony under the dog's grip. Heathcliff picks up a stone and tries to thrust it between the dog's jaws

Get the filthy beast off her. I'll kill it! I'll damn well smash its teeth!
Servant Keep fast, Skulker, keep fast!
Mr Linton What, prey?
Servant Skulker has caught a little girl, sir.
Mr Linton Ler her loose.

The Servant pulls Skulker off

Servant And there's a lad here who looks an out-and-outer. (*He grabs hold of Heathcliff*)
Heathcliff We are ——
Servant Hold your tongue, you foul-mouthed thief. Mr Linton, sir, don't lay down your gun!
Mr Linton The villain scowls so it would be a kindness to the county to hang him at once before he shows his nature in acts as well as features.
Isabella Frightful thing! Put him in the cellar, Papa. He's exactly like the fortune teller that stole my tame pheasant, isn't he, Edgar?
Edgar I'll say.
Cathy (*laughing*) You've seen us at church. Don't you know who we are?
Edgar That's Miss Earnshaw! And look how Skulker has bitten her, how her foot bleeds!
Mr Linton Miss Earnshaw — scouring the country with a gypsy! What carelessness in her brother! I've heard from the curate that he lets her grow up in absolute heathenism. Her companion is that strange acquisition my late neighbour made in his journey to Liverpool. A wicked boy at all events and quite unfit for a decent house. Carry the girl in.

Cathy turns back to look at Heathcliff and smiles. The Servant carries her in and the family follow

Heathcliff is excluded

Heathcliff I returned to my station as spy because if Catherine had wished to return I intended shattering their great glass pane into a million fragments. (*He rejoins Nelly*) She sat quietly by the fire. They dried and combed her beautiful hair. I left her, as merry as could be, kindling a spark of spirit in the empty blue eyes of the Lintons. I saw them full of stupid admiration. She is so immeasurably superior to them, to everybody on earth, is she not, Nelly?

Nelly There will come more of this business than you reckon on. (*She blows out the candle*) You're incurable, Heathcliff, and Mr Hindley will have to proceed to extremities. You see if he won't.

Nelly pushes Heathcliff along to retire

The Lights fade to Black-out

SCENE 6

Wuthering Heights. Daytime

Hindley, Frances, Heathcliff and Nelly assemble, awaiting Cathy's arrival. Heathcliff hangs back. The sound of a carriage can be heard

Frances Here she is! We have waited months for this, Nelly!
Hindley No need for hysterics, Frances.

Cathy enters. She seems to have grown up and become a sophisticated lady

Hindley Why, Cathy, you are quite a beauty. I should not have known you. You look like a lady. Isabella Linton is not to be compared with her, is she Frances?
Frances Isabella has not her natural advantages. But you must not grow wild again here, Cathy. Ellen, help Miss Catherine off with her things. (*To Cathy*) Let me untie your hat. You will disarrange your curls.

Nelly takes Cathy's cloak, revealing the beautiful dress she is wearing

Cathy Ellen, come here and let me kiss you.
Nelly I'm all flour. I've been making the Christmas cake, miss.
Cathy Where is Heathcliff? (*She takes off her gloves*)
Hindley Heathcliff, you may come forward and wish Miss Catherine welcome like the other servants.

Cathy catches sight of Heathcliff and runs to him and kisses him. She then stops, draws back and bursts out laughing

Cathy How very black and cross you look! How funny and grim. But that's because I'm used to the Lintons. Well, Heathcliff, have you forgotten me?

Hindley Shake hands, Heathcliff, I permit you.

Heathcliff I shall not. I shall not be laughed at, I shall not bear it.

Heathcliff turns to break from the circle but Cathy seizes him

Cathy I didn't mean to laugh at you. I couldn't help myself. Heathcliff, shake hands at least. Why are you sulking? It was only that you looked odd. If you wash your face and brush your hair it will be all right. But you are so dirty!

Heathcliff (*freeing himself from Cathy*) You needn't have touched me. I shall be as dirty as I please. I like to be dirty!

Heathcliff rushes aside

Cathy What have I said to deserve such a display of bad temper?

Frances Never mind him. You are home, Cathy, we have you back at Wuthering Heights at last.

Frances and Cathy exit

The Lights fade to Black-out

Scene 7

The same. Christmas Eve

Nelly is stirring apple sauce as Heathcliff enters

Heathcliff Nelly, make me decent. I'm going to be good.

Nelly High time, Heathcliff. You have grieved Catherine. She's sorry she ever came home. It looked as if you envied her because she is thought more of than you.

Heathcliff I, envy Catherine, when everything I have is hers? Did she say she was grieved?

Nelly She cried when I told her you were off again this morning.

Heathcliff I cried last night and I had more reason.

Nelly Proud people breed sad sorrows for themselves. You must ask pardon when she comes in. Come here. I'll brush you up so when Edgar Linton comes for dinner, he shall look a doll beside you. You are younger but you are twice as broad across the shoulders. You could knock him down in a twinkling.

Heathcliff But Nelly, if I knocked him down twenty times that wouldn't make him less handsome. I wish I had his light hair and fair skin and had a chance of being as rich.

Nelly And cried for Mama at every turn! Come to the glass. (*She brings Heathcliff to face the audience; looking in a mimed mirror*) Do you mark your eyes like a couple of black fiends, who never open their windows boldly but lurk glinting like the devil's spies? Learn to raise your lids frankly and change the fiends to confident, innocent angels.

Heathcliff In other words I must wish for Edgar Linton's great blue eyes. I do, but that won't help me to get them.

Nelly A good heart will help you to a bonny face, my lad. (*Washing Heathcliff's face with a cloth and brushing his hair*) Who knows, but your father was the emperor of China and your mother an Indian queen, each of them able to buy up with one week's income Wuthering Heights and the Grange together? Who knows, but you were kidnapped by wicked sailors and brought to England. Were I in your place I would frame high notions of my birth and the thoughts of what I was would give me courage. (*She finishes washing and combing him*) There now, tell me whether you don't think yourself rather handsome?

Nelly shows Heathcliff the mirror and he smiles. There is sound of a carriage

Be there to meet them and be friendly.

Hindley, Joseph, Cathy, Edgar and Isabella enter

Hindley (*indicating Heathcliff*) Keep him out of the room. Send him into the garret until dinner is over. He'll be cramming his fingers into the tarts and stealing the fruit.

Nelly Nay, sir, he'll touch nothing. And I suppose he must have his share of the dainties as well as we?

Hindley He shall have his share of my hand if I catch him downstairs again 'til dark. Be gone, you vagabond!

Nelly He has cleaned himself up, to meet the guests.

Hindley You can't make a thoroughbred out of a plough horse.

Edgar Quite hideous. Do we have to look at him while we eat? It may restrict my capacity to swallow.

Isabella laughs. Heathcliff reaches for the pot of apple sauce and tips it over Edgar's head. Edgar lets out a wail

Hindley You'll pay for that, you cur!

Hindley beats Heathcliff and bundles him out of the room

Nelly roughly cleans up Edgar as Isabella weeps

Edgar What did I do?
Cathy You should not have spoken to him, Edgar! He was in a bad temper and now he'll be flogged. I hate him to be flogged! Why did you speak to him?
Edgar (*sobbing*) I didn't. I promised Mama I wouldn't say one word to him and I didn't.
Isabella (*sobbing*) He didn't. I heard him and he didn't.
Cathy Well, don't cry. You're not killed. Don't make more mischief, my brother is coming. Be quiet! Give over, Isabella! Has anybody hurt you?

Hindley enters

Hindley There, there, children. That brute has warmed me nicely. Next time, Master Edgar, take the law into your own fists. Stop crying now.

Edgar and Isabella cry harder

Look, here's the Gimmerton band to sing us carols.

Joseph enters

Joseph The devil's psalmody!

The Band enter and begin to sing

The whole household gathers. They sing a verse of the carol "God Rest Ye Merry Gentlemen"

Cathy sneaks away and stands before Heathcliff's door, which can be staged using the frame of the skylight

Heathcliff appears

Cathy Heathcliff? Heathcliff? Won't you speak to me? Let me in. Aren't I Cathy? Open the door or I'll climb over the roof and get in by the skylight. Nothing will keep me out.
Heathcliff Go back to your friends. What do you want with me?

Cathy Do you think I could eat a mouthful knowing that you were hungry? All evening I wearied to find an opportunity to come to you. I struggled to keep the tears from my eyes but they would come, burning, knowing you suffered alone. I have been in purgatory.

Heathcliff I have been alone. You have been with them.

Cathy Don't speak to me like that, Heathcliff. Without you I am only half myself and what is that? An abandoned nest found on the moors, the chicks starved of life.

Heathcliff opens the door

Heathcliff People talk of happiness. I'd say they're speaking gibberish if there wasn't you, Cathy.

Cathy The guests have gone. Come down with me now, warm yourself by the fire. Nelly will give you something.

They exit

The Lights fade to Black-out

SCENE 8

The same. Later that evening

Heathcliff has a plate of food which Nelly has given him. He tosses his food aside

Heathcliff I am trying to settle how I shall pay Hindley back. I don't care how long it takes, if only he doesn't die before I can do it.

Nelly For shame, Heathcliff. It's for God to punish wicked people. We should learn to forgive.

Heathcliff No. God won't have the satisfaction that I shall. I only wish I knew the best way. While I'm thinking of that I don't feel any pain.

Heathcliff kicks his chair over and runs out

Nelly (*to Lockwood*) But Mr Lockwood, these tales cannot divert you. How could I dream of chattering on at such a rate and you nodding for bed.

Lockwood Just another half hour!

Nelly The clock is on the stroke of eleven, sir.

Lockwood No matter, I never sleep 'til one or two. Then I wake at ten.

Nelly Ten! That's the prime of the morning gone. A person who's not done half their work by ten risks leaving the other half undone.

Lockwood You forget I'm a gentleman.

Nelly Oh, yes.

Lockwood Mrs Dean, you tell the story in just the method I like. Excepting a few provincialisms of slight consequence, you have no marks of the manners peculiar to your class.

Nelly There's nothing peculiar about *my* class.

Lockwood I only meant that I'm sure you think a great deal more than most servants.

Nelly We servants think, only we don't always let on what we think.

Lockwood Exactly. You have been compelled to cultivate your reflective faculties for want of occasions, for frittering your life away in silly trifles, like trips to the theatre. I perceive that people in these semi-barbaric northern regions acquire over people in towns the value that a spider in a dungeon does over a spider in a cottage. Do you see?

Nelly I'd better pass on. The summer of 1778, nearly twenty-three years ago …

Frances and Hindley enter. Hindley holds a baby and Frances is consumptive and feverish

Nelly approaches them

Frances Nelly. Isn't he the finest lad that ever breathed? Such joy.

Hindley Our Hareton.

Nelly How's the mistress? Doctor says ——

Hindley Damn the doctor! Frances will be perfectly well by this time next week.

Frances You must nurse him, Nelly, 'til I am better. (*She collapses*)

Hindley Frances!

Hindley hands Nelly the baby and picks up Frances, who puts her arms about his neck and faints

Frances!

Hindley rushes off carrying Frances

Nelly After the mistress died, the child fell wholly into my hands. Hindley was desperate. He neither wept nor prayed. He drank.

Hindley enters and sits at the table with a bottle

If you could have seen what an infernal house we had!

Hindley exits

The Lights fade to Black-out

SCENE 9

The same

Heathcliff, Nelly and the baby are on stage

Cathy enters

Cathy Fix my hair, Nelly.

Nelly begins on her hair. Heathcliff watches

Heathcliff Cathy? Are you going anywhere?
Cathy No, it's raining.
Heathcliff Why have you that silk frock on? Nobody coming here, I hope?
Cathy Not that I know of. You should be in the field now, Heathcliff.
Heathcliff Hindley has freed us from his accursed presence for once. I'll not work any more today, I'll stay with you.
Cathy Isabella and Edgar Linton talked of calling this afternoon. As it rains I hardly expect them, but they may come and if they do you run the risk of being scolded.
Heathcliff Order Ellen to say you are engaged, Cathy. Don't turn me out for those pitiful friends of yours.
Cathy Oh, Nelly, you've combed my hair quite out of curl!
Heathcliff Look at the almanac on the wall. The crosses are for the evenings you have spent with the Lintons and the dots for those spent with me. Do you see? I've marked every day.
Cathy Yes, very foolish. As if I took notice. Should I always be sitting with you? What good do I get? What do you talk about? You might be dumb or a baby for anything you say to amuse me.
Heathcliff You never told me before that I talked too little or you disliked my company, Cathy.
Cathy It is no company when people know nothing and say nothing.

Heathcliff exits, angry and hurt

Heathcliff ...

Nelly picks up a duster and goes about her work

   Edgar enters

Edgar I'm not come too soon, am I?
Cathy No, Edgar. What are you doing here, Nelly?
Nelly My work, miss.
Cathy Take yourself and your dusters off. When company are in the house servants don't commence scouring and cleaning in the same room.
Nelly It's a good oppourtunity now the master is away. I'm sure Mr Edgar will excuse me.
Cathy But I will not. (*She snatches the duster from Nelly's hand and pinches her spitefully*)
Nelly Oh miss, that's a nasty trick. You have no right to nip me. I won't bear it.
Cathy I didn't touch you, you lying creature.
Nelly What's that then? (*She shows her bruise*)
Cathy (*stamping her foot*) Leave the room, Ellen.

The baby begins to cry. Cathy picks him up and shoves him at Nelly

   Get out and take that squaller with you!
Nelly Miss Catherine! (*She snatches Hareton back from Cathy*)
Edgar Catherine, love! Catherine.

Edgar tries to stop Cathy. She slaps his face. After a pause, Edgar reaches for his coat

Nelly That's right, take warning and be gone! Now you've had a glimpse of her true nature.
Cathy Where are you going?

Edgar attempts to leave

   You must not go.
Edgar I must and I shall.
Cathy No, not yet, Edgar Linton. Sit down. You shall not leave me in that temper. I should be miserable all night and I won't be miserable for you.
Edgar Can I stay after you have struck me? You've made me afraid and ashamed of you. I'll not come here again.
Cathy Well, go if you please. Get away. And now I'll cry. I'll cry myself sick.

Nelly Miss is dreadfully wayward, sir. As bad as any marred child. You
better be riding home before she makes herself sick to grieve us.
Edgar Cathy. Cathy.

He holds her hands. Cathy looks up into his face

Cathy.
Nelly (*looking at Edgar*) Doomed.

*A drunk Hindley can be heard arriving home. Dogs are heard barking
and Hindley swears*

Nelly That's Mr Earnshaw, home rabid drunk. Take Mr Edgar out the
kitchen way.
Cathy Quickly.

The baby cries

Cathy and Edgar exit

Nelly looks for somewhere to hide the baby and puts him in a cupboard

Hindley enters, holding a knife

Hindley Where is he?
Nelly Who?
Hindley That hideous little villain, Hareton, my son. Unnatural cub! He
deserves flaying alive for not running to greet me.
Nelly He's a baby!
Hindley Where is he? Tell me or with the help of Satan I'll make you
swallow this carving knife.
Nelly I don't like the carving knife, Mr Hindley. It's been cutting
herrings. I'd rather be shot, if you please.
Hindley You'd rather be damned.

*Hindley grabs Nelly and pushes the knife at her teeth. They struggle
and she spits it out. Hindley releases her, then hears Hareton cry and
discovers him*

Hush child, hush, there's a joy. Kiss me. What? It won't! Damn thee!
I'll break the brat's neck.

*Hindley grabs the crying baby and runs upstairs. Nelly chases them.
Lockwood jumps up from his seat and joins in*

Nelly No, you don't know what you're about, Mr Hindley.

Hindley stands at the top of the stairs and holds the baby over the banister

Oh, save us.

Heathcliff enters as Hindley drops the baby. Nelly screams

Lockwood Good heavens!

Heathcliff catches the baby

Nelly Thank God.
Hindley It's your fault, Ellen. You should have kept him out of sight. Is he injured?
Nelly If he's not killed, he'll be an idiot …

Nelly takes the baby from Heathcliff, who looks aghast that he has saved his enemy's child

Heathcliff Is it Hareton? I've saved him! Damn it!
Hindley Let me see him.
Nelly You've terrified the poor bairn. A pretty state you've come to.
Hindley I shall come to prettier yet! (*He grabs a bottle of brandy*)
Nelly Nay don't, Mr Hindley. Take pity on this unfortunate boy if you care nothing for yourself.
Hindley Anyone will do better for him than I shall.
Nelly Have mercy on your own soul, then.
Hindley Not I, I'll send it to hell to punish its maker.

Hindley drinks, then exits

Heathcliff It's a pity he cannot kill himself with drink.
Nelly He's doing his best.

The Lights fade to Black-out

SCENE 10

A rainy evening

Heathcliff lies down on a bench, concealed. Nelly is calming Hareton

Nelly (*singing*) It was far in the night, and the bairnies grat,
　　　　　　　　　　The mither beneath the mools heard that.

Cathy enters

Cathy Are you alone, Nelly?
Nelly Yes, miss.
Cathy Where's Heathcliff?
Nelly About his work in the stable.
Cathy Nelly, will you keep a secret for me?
Nelly Is it worth keeping?
Cathy Edgar Linton has asked me to marry him and I've given him an
　　answer. Tell me which you think it ought to have been.

*Heathcliff comes out and stands in the shadows unseen by Catherine but
noticed by Nelly*

Nelly Really, Miss Catherine, how can I know?
Cathy I accepted him, Nelly. Be quick and say if I was wrong.
Nelly You accepted him! What good is discussing it?
Cathy Say.
Nelly Do you love Mr Edgar?
Cathy Of course I do. Who wouldn't?

Heathcliff registers this like a blow

Nelly Why?
Cathy Because he is young and cheerful.
Nelly Bad.
Cathy And because he loves me and he will be rich and I shall be the
　　greatest woman of the neighbourhood.
Nelly Worse! There are several other such young men in the world,
　　what should hinder you from loving them?
Cathy If there be any, they are out of my way. I have only seen Edgar.
　　I have only to do with the present.
Nelly Well that settles it. If you have only to do with the present, marry
　　him.
Cathy I shall marry him but you have not told me whether I'm right.
Nelly Perfectly right; if people be right to marry only for the present.
　　You will escape a disorderly, comfortless home for a respectable one.
　　You love Edgar, he loves you, all seems smooth and easy. Where is
　　the obstacle?

Cathy Here. (*She strikes her forehead*) And here (*She strikes her breast*). In whichever place the soul lives. In my soul and in my heart I'm convinced I'm wrong.

Heathcliff makes a move towards Cathy

Nelly, do you never dream queer dreams? I've dreamt dreams that have stayed with me ever after. They've gone through and through me like wine through water and changed the colour of my thoughts. If I were in heaven, Nelly, I should be extremely miserable.

Nelly Because you are not fit to go there. All sinners would be miserable in heaven.

Cathy I dreamt once that I was there.

Nelly I tell you, I won't harken to your dreams, Miss Catherine, I'll go to bed.

Cathy I was only going to say that heaven did not seem my home and I broke my heart with weeping to come back to earth and the angels were so angry that they flung me out into the middle of the heath on the top of Wuthering Heights where I woke sobbing for joy. I've no more business to marry Edgar Linton than I have to be in heaven and if my wicked brother had not brought Heathcliff so low, I shouldn't have thought of it. Now, it would degrade me to marry Heathcliff.

Nelly Miss Catherine!

Heathcliff leaves in distress

Nelly hesitates but does not stop him

Cathy So he shall never know how I love him. He's more myself than I am. Whatever our souls are made of, his and mine are the same and Edgar is as different from ours as frost from fire.

Nelly Pity Heathcliff, if he loves you. How will he bear the separation?

Cathy Who is to separate us? Not as long as I live. Nelly, you think I am a selfish wretch but if Heathcliff and I were married we should be beggars, whereas if I marry Edgar I can aid Heathcliff's rise.

Nelly With your husband's money, Miss Catherine?

Cathy Surely you and everyone has a notion that there is an existence of yours beyond you. Mine is Heathcliff. My great thought in living is him. If all else perished and he remained I should still continue to be, and if all else remained and he were annihilated the universe should turn into a mighty stranger. My love for Edgar will change as winter changes trees, but my love for Heathcliff is the eternal rock beneath. I am Heathcliff. He's always, always in my mind.

Nelly He was listening, Miss Cathy.

Cathy stops

He heard a good part of what you said. Then he quit the place just as
you said how Hindley had brought him so low.

Cathy Why didn't you tell me he was there? What did I say Nelly? I've
forgotten. Tell me what I've said to grieve him? (*Calling*) Heathcliff!
(*She pauses*) Why doesn't he come?

Nelly What a trifle scares you. Heathcliff's taken a saunter on the moors
in the moonlight. No great cause for alarm.

Cathy (*pacing*) Where can he be? What did I say?

Joseph enters

Joseph In't Heathcliff comed in frough th'field be this time? What is he
abaht? Girt eedle seeght! Yon lad gets war un' war. E'll go t'divil.

Cathy I'll find him. (*Calling*) Heathcliff!

Cathy exits into the rain

(*Off; calling*) Heathcliff!

Nelly (*calling after Cathy*) Are you bent on getting your death? Do
you know what clock it is? Past twelve. No use waiting longer on that
foolish boy. He'll have gone to Gimmerton and he'll stay there now.

Cathy enters

Joseph Nay nay, he's noan at Gimmerton. Aw's never wonder bud
he's at t'bothom of a bog hoile. Thank hivin for that. Miss, yah muh
be t'next.

Hindley enters

Hindley What ails you, Cathy? You look dismal as a drowned whelp.
Why are you so damp and pale, child? What took you into the rain?

Joseph Running after t'lads, as usuald! It's bonny behaviour, lurking
amang t'fields after twelve ut night wi'that fahl divil uf a gypsy,
Heathcliff!

Cathy Silence.

Hindley Were you with Heathcliff? Speak the truth. Though I hate him
as much as ever, he did me a good turn a short time since and that
will make my conscience tender of breaking his neck. I'll dismiss him
instead.

Cathy If you do turn him out of doors I'll go with him — but perhaps you'll never have the opportunity, perhaps he's gone for ever. (*She bursts into tears*)
Hindley Go to your room, Cathy.
Cathy (*running to the front door*) Heathcliff!

Hindley and Joseph drag Cathy to the bedroom as she struggles, protests and cries

The Lights cross fade

SCENE 11

Nelly and Lockwood are on stage

Nelly I thought she was going mad. I sent for the doctor. It was delirium and the onset of fever. He bled her and told us to take care she did not throw herself from the window. Old Mrs Linton came and took Cathy to the Grange. The poor dame had reason to repent her kindness. She and her husband both took the fever and died. Our young lady returned to us. Saucier than ever. Once when she provoked me exceedingly, I laid the blame for Heathcliff's disappearance on her — for it was her fault.
Lockwood Without a doubt.
Nelly For months she wouldn't speak to me except as a servant to order about. She married the infatuated Edgar Linton at Gimmerton Chapel.
Lockwood He had his hands full.

Cathy and Edgar appear framed as if at a church door

Nelly He believed himself the happiest man alive.

Cathy and Edgar kiss and the frame breaks

Well, it's midnight.
Lockwood Don't stop there, Nelly. I'll be tossing and turning all night. I have an exceedingly active and curious mind which you may attribute to my excessive intellectual abilities. Did Heathcliff earn a fortune in America or did he go to Cambridge University and come back a gentleman?
Nelly You should take your medicine, Mr Lockwood.

Lockwood Have pity on a man stuck here with only pills, powders and leeches for company. Yourself excluded, Mrs Dean.

Nelly Goodnight, Mr Lockwood.

Lockwood I supplicate myself to you, Nelly.

Nelly Just 'til half-past.

Lockwood Thank you.

Nelly (*sitting*) I went with Miss Catherine to the Grange. To my disappointment, she behaved infinitely better than I expected.

Inside Thrushcross Grange, Cathy and Edgar sit awaiting tea

One mellow September evening I was collecting apples in the garden when I heard a voice behind me say ...

Heathcliff appears

Heathcliff Nelly, is that you? I have waited here an hour. All around has been as still as death. You do not know me? Look, I'm not a stranger.

Nelly What! You've come back? Is it really you?

Heathcliff Where is she, Nelly? I want to have one word with her, your mistress.

Nelly It is you — altered but ... have you been for a soldier?

Heathcliff Go, say some person from Gimmerton wishes to speak to her. I am in hell 'til you do.

Heathcliff waits, while Nelly goes to where Cathy sits with Edgar

Nelly (*to Cathy*) A person from Gimmerton wishes to see you, ma'am.

Cathy What does he want?

Nelly I didn't ask.

Cathy Draw the curtains and bring up tea, Nelly. I'll be back directly.

Cathy remains on stage. We see her meeting Heathcliff as the scene continues

Edgar Who was it?

Nelly Someone the mistress does not expect — that Heathcliff. You remember, sir, he used to live at the Heights.

Edgar The gypsy ploughboy! What the devil does he want?

Cathy returns to the scene

Cathy Edgar, Edgar! Heathcliff's come back. (*She embraces Edgar*)

Edgar Don't strangle me for it. He never struck me as such a marvellous treasure.

Cathy For my sake, be friends now. I've asked him to come up.

Edgar To the parlour?

Cathy Where else?

Edgar Try to be glad without being absurd, Catherine. The whole household need not witness the sight of your welcoming a runaway servant as a brother.

Heathcliff enters the scene. He and Cathy stare at each other

Nelly Heathcliff had grown into a tall, athletic, well-formed man.

Lockwood I suppose that is to some tastes.

Nelly Catherine kept her gaze fixed on him as if she feared he might vanish.

Edgar Sit down, sir. Mrs Linton would have me give you a cordial reception and I always wish to please her.

Cathy I shall think it a dream tomorrow. Cruel Heathcliff, you don't deserve this welcome. To be absent and silent for three years and never to think of me.

Heathcliff A little more than you thought of me. I heard of your marriage, Cathy, not long since and I had a plan — just to get one more glimpse of your face, settle my score with Hindley, and then prevent the law by doing execution on myself. Your welcome has put these ideas out of my head. Nay, you'll not drive me off again. You were really sorry for me, were you? Well, there was cause. I've fought through a bitter life since I last heard your voice, and you must forgive me because I struggled only for you.

Edgar Catherine, unless we are to have cold tea you must come to the table.

Catherine does not move

Are you staying in Gimmerton, Mr Heathcliff?

Heathcliff No, Wuthering Heights. Mr Earnshaw invited me when I called this morning.

Edgar Hindley invited you! There was no love lost between you as I remember.

Cathy and Heathcliff continue to stare at each other

Aren't you eating or drinking, Catherine? Mrs Linton!

Heathcliff I'll come tomorrow.

Heathcliff bows and leaves

Cathy stares after him

Edgar I'll come tomorrow? Are we to see him every day?
Cathy Heathcliff is now worthy of anyone's regard. It would honour
  the first gentleman of the country to be his friend.
Edgar I'm feeling unwell, Cathy.
Cathy Stop sulking, Edgar.
Edgar It's selfish of you to chatter on while I decline.
Cathy Don't cloud my joy with idle petulance, Edgar. Goodnight.

Cathy exits

Edgar (*groaning*) Nelly, Nelly. I may be in need of salts. (*He looks for
  Nelly; robustly*) Nelly!

Edgar stalks off

Nelly He had a new source of misfortune.

The Lights fade to Black-out

SCENE 12

Isabella is alone, crying

Cathy enters. She is now visibly pregnant

Cathy Isabella. What is making you unhappy?
Isabella You are. You are too harsh.
Cathy When have I been harsh, naughty fondling? Tell me!
Isabella Yesterday. And now.
Cathy Yesterday?
Isabella In our walk along the moor. You told me to ramble where I
  pleased while you sauntered on with Mr Heathcliff.
Cathy You could have kept with us if you'd wanted. I thought
  Heathcliff's talk would have nothing entertaining for you.
Isabella Oh, no! You kept me away because you knew I liked to be
  there.
Cathy Are you sane, Isabella?

Isabella I wanted …

Cathy Well?

Isabella I wanted to be with him! And I won't always be sent off! You are a dog in a manger, Cathy, and you desire no one to be loved but yourself.

Cathy You impertinent little monkey! Surely you don't covet Heathcliff's admiration, or think he's an agreeable person? Tell me I'm mistaken.

Isabella No. I love him. I love him more than you ever loved Edgar and he might love me if you let him.

Catherine I wouldn't be you for a kingdom then. (*To Nelly*) Nelly, tell her what Heathcliff is — an unreclaimed creature, a pitiless, wolfish man. He'd crush you like a sparrow's egg. He couldn't love a Linton, but he'd marry you for your fortune. That's my picture and I'm his friend.

Isabella For shame! You are worse than twenty foes.

Cathy You think I speak from wickedness?

Isabella Yes, and I shudder at you.

Cathy Good. Try for yourself then, if that's your spirit. I have done with you.

Nelly He's a bird of bad omen. They say Hindley is worse and worse since he came. They sit up at nights gambling, drinking. Hindley has mortgaged his land.

Isabella You are in league with the rest, Ellen. I'll not listen to your slanders!

Heathcliff enters

Heathcliff What slanders are they?

Cathy Heathcliff, I'm proud to show you — at last somebody that dotes on you more than myself.

Heathcliff looks at Nelly

Nay, it is not Nelly, don't look at her. My poor little sister-in-law is breaking her heart by mere contemplation of your moral and physical beauty. It lies in your power to be Edgar's brother!

Isabella tries to run off but Cathy grabs her

No, Isabella, you shan't run off! We were quarrelling like cats about you. I was informed that if I but had the manners to stand aside, my rival, as she would have herself, would shoot a shaft into your soul and send my image into eternal oblivion.

Isabella Catherine. I thank you not to slander me, even in a joke. Mr Heathcliff, be kind enough to bid your friend release me.

Cathy No. I'll not be called a dog in a manger again. Heathcliff, why don't you look pleased at my news?

Heathcliff I think you belie her. She wishes to be out of my society now, at any rate.

Isabella struggles to be free and digs her nails into Cathy's hand. Cathy reacts, releases Isabella and tends to her hand

Cathy There's a tigress. Be gone, for God's sake. Hide your vixen face. Heathcliff, you'd better beware your eyes.

Heathcliff I'd wrench her nails from her fingers if they ever menaced me.

Isabella runs off with a sob

Cathy She's been pining for you for weeks. But don't notice it further. I wanted to punish her sauciness, that's all. I like her too much to let you seize her up and devour her.

Heathcliff And I like her too little to attempt it. If I lived alone with that waxen face I would be painting it the colours of the rainbow, turning the blue eyes black. She's her brother's heir, is she not?

Cathy Half a dozen nephews will erase her title, please heaven! Let's walk.

Cathy and Heathcliff exit

The Lights fade to Black-out

SCENE 13

Thrushcross Grange

Isabella walks along the corridors of the house. Heathcliff emerges from the shadows. They regard each other. She covers his hands in kisses. They embrace each other and kiss

Nelly enters

Nelly Judas! Traitor! Hypocrite! Deceiver!

Cathy hurries in

Cathy Nelly?

Isabella tears herself free and runs away

Nelly Your worthless friend! The sneaking rascal yonder. Making love
to Miss Isabella when he told you he hated her!
Cathy You are not the mistress here, Nelly. Keep to your place.

Nelly exits

Heathcliff, what are you about? I said you must let Isabella alone,
unless you are tired of being received here and want Edgar to draw the
bolts against you.
Heathcliff Let him try it. Every day I grow madder for sending him to
heaven.
Cathy Hush. Why have you disregarded my request? Did she come
across you on purpose?
Heathcliff What is it to you? I have a right to kiss her. I'm not your
husband. You needn't be jealous of me.
Cathy I'm not jealous of you — I'm jealous for you. Don't scowl at me.
If you like Isabella you shall marry her. But do you like her? Tell me
the truth. (*She pauses*) You don't love her.
Heathcliff You have treated me infernally, Cathy, do you hear? And if
you flatter yourself that I don't perceive it, you are a fool. And if you
think I can be consoled by sweet words, you are an idiot. And if you
fancy, I'll suffer unrevenged, I'll convince you of the contrary in a
very little while. Meanwhile, thank you for telling me your sister-in-
law's secret. I swear I'll make the most of it.
Cathy How will you, ungrateful brute?
Heathcliff I seek no revenge on you. You are allowed to torture me to
death for your own amusement, only allow me to amuse myself in the
same style. If I really thought you wished me to marry Isabella, I'd
cut my throat.
Cathy The evil is that I'm not jealous, is it? Edgar agreed to your coming
here and just as I began to be secure, you deceive his sister. If you
quarrel with Edgar you'll revenge yourself on me most efficiently.
Nelly (*to Lockwood*) I thought it best to inform Mr Edgar of what was
occurring in his own house.

Edgar enters

(*To Edgar*) I discovered Heathcliff with Miss Isabella in the kitchen
garden, sir.
Edgar Yes?
Nelly *With* her, sir!
Edgar Good God!

Nelly (*calling after him*) I thought you ought to know. He's with Miss Catherine as we speak.

Edgar Catherine. What notion of propriety must you have to talk to this blackguard?

Cathy Have you been listening at the door, Edgar?

Edgar (*to Heathcliff*) Sir, your presence is a moral poison, especially as regards Isabella, my sister. For that reason I shall deny you, hereafter, admission to this house and give notice, now, that I require your instant departure.

Heathcliff By God, Mr Linton, I'm mortally sorry you are not worth the knocking down.

Cathy If you have not the courage to attack him, make an apology or allow yourself to be beaten. I was defending you and yours, Edgar. I wish Heathcliff may flog you sick for thinking evil of me.

Edgar (*tottering and leaning against a chair*) Oh, heavens!

Cathy Cheer up, you shan't be hurt.

Heathcliff That is the shivering, slavering thing you preferred to me? Is he going to faint with fear?

Edgar lashes out unexpectedly, catching Heathcliff. Edgar collapses

Cathy (*to Heathcliff*) There! Now, you've done with coming here — get away.

Heathcliff By hell, no! I'll crush his ribs like a rotten hazelnut. If I don't hit him now I will murder him later.

Nelly He already sent for the coachmen and two gardeners with bludgeons. I see them coming now.

Cathy Make haste.

Heathcliff exits

Nelly (*to Lockwood*) No one was coming. I framed a bit of a lie there, thinking it for the best.

Lockwood Quick thinking, Mrs Dean.

Edgar comes round

Edgar He is gone then. I shall not stay. But I wish to learn after this evening's events whether you wish to continue your intimacy with —

Cathy Oh, for mercy's sake let us hear no more of it now.

Edgar To get rid of me, answer my question. Will you give up Heathcliff or me? It is impossible to be my friend and his at the same time. I require to know which one you choose.

Cathy Let me alone. Don't you see I can scarcely stand! (*She dashes her fists against her head*)
Edgar Fetch some water, Nelly.

Cathy's fit continues. Nelly gets some water and sprinkles it on Cathy but she becomes deathly still

She has blood on her lips.
Nelly Never mind. This is an act. She has decided in advance to get her own way. We must leave her, sir. It's for the best.

Nelly and Edgar leave Cathy alone in the room

Cathy Nelly.

Nelly enters

A thousand smith's hammers are beating in my head. What made Edgar turn listener? I could have soon diverted Heathcliff from Isabella — the rest meant nothing. Well, if I cannot keep Heathcliff for my friend, if Edgar will be mean and jealous, I will break their hearts by breaking my own. And Nelly, if you see Edgar, say to him I am in danger of being seriously ill. Do it, my good Nelly.

Nelly passes by Edgar

Edgar I should go to her.
Nelly Best you leave her, sir. There is nothing in the world the matter but temper which cures itself.

They exit except Cathy, who paces in the extremity of her anxiety

Cathy Heathcliff! My heart will break.

The Lights fade to Black-out

ACT II
SCENE 1

Outside Thrushcross Grange

Lockwood Another night over and I am so many days nearer health and spring. God, the north is dreary! But people must live somewhere. They cannot all be in London. Mrs Dean broke off at a most inconvenient point. Her story is not exactly what I would have chosen to amuse me, but never mind! I'll extract wholesome medicine from its bitter herbs. Let me beware of the fascination that lurks in Catherine Heathcliff's brilliant eyes. What a curious fix I'd be in if I surrendered my heart and the daughter turned out to be a second edition of the mother! Whoa!

Nelly enters with gruel

Nelly How are you this morning, Mr Lockwood?
Lockwood Continue your tale immediately, Mrs Dean.
Nelly I said how are you?
Lockwood Much better thank you, Nelly.
Nelly Here. Eat this. (*She spoons him some gruel*)
Lockwood It looks like gruel!
Nelly It is gruel.
Lockwood Goodness it's ... wholesome. Do people actually eat this?
Nelly The sensible ones. Three days went by and Cathy wouldn't touch a morsel.

Nelly joins Cathy in her room. She has brought some gruel for her

Try some.
Cathy I won't touch it. I will die since no one cares anything about me. What is that apathetic being doing? Has he fallen into lethargy or is he dead?
Nelly If you mean Mr Edgar, he's tolerably well. His studies occupy him, he is continually among his books.
Cathy Among his books! And I am on the brink of the grave! Can you not inform him?
Nelly Of what, ma'am?
Cathy That I am about to starve to death.

Nelly Why ma'am, the master had no idea of your being deranged, so he does not fear that you will die of hunger.

Cathy Tell him. Persuade him I will! These awful nights. I've never closed my lids and oh, I've been tormented. I've been haunted, Nelly.

Nelly begins to leave

But I begin to fancy you don't like me. How strange. I thought, though everyone despised each other, they could not help loving me. And now they have all turned enemies. How dreary to meet death surrounded by their cold faces. (*She begins tearing up her pillow, naming the feathers*) That's a wild duck's and that's a moorcock's ... and this — I'd know it among thousands — a lapwing's. The lapwing is a bonny bird, wheeling over our heads in the middle of the moor, it wanted to get to its nest. It felt rain coming. This feather — (*holding up a feather*) — was picked up from the heath, the bird was not shot, we saw its nest in winter full of little skeletons. Heathcliff set a trap over it and the old ones dared not come home. I made him promise never to shoot a lapwing after that. Did he shoot my lapwings, Nelly?

Nelly Lie down and shut your eyes, you're wandering. There's a mess. Give over with that baby work. The down is flying about like snow.

Nelly collects the feathers

Cathy I see in you, Nelly, an aged woman. You have grey hair and bent shoulders. This bed is the fairy cave under Peniston Cragg and you are gathering elf-bolts to hurt our heifers. I'm not wandering or else I should believe you are that withered hag. (*She starts*) I see a face! Don't you see it?

Nelly That's a mirror, miss.

Cathy Will it come out when you are gone? Oh, Nelly, this room is haunted.

Nelly There's nobody there. It was yourself, Mrs Linton. See yourself in it standing next to me. (*She shows Cathy herself in the mirror*)

Cathy (*shrieking*) Dreadful!

Nelly Who's the coward now?

Cathy I don't know myself. My brain got confused. Stay with me. I dread sleeping. My dreams appall me.

Nelly A sound sleep would do you good, ma'am.

Cathy How long is it since I shut myself in here?

Nelly Since Monday. It's now Thursday night.

Cathy That brief time?

Nelly Long enough to live on nothing but cold water and ill temper.

Cathy I tell you what I thought as I lay here. That I was at home, at Wuthering Heights in my old bed, and the wind was sounding in the firs, coming straight down from the moors. The last seven years of my life drew a blank. I forgot they had been at all. I was a child, my father just buried and my heart ached with some great grief. It was the separation that Hindley had ordered between me and Heathcliff. I was laid alone for the first time and when I woke from a dismal doze after a night of weeping I found myself here. Supposing at twelve years old I had been wrenched from the Heights and been converted at a stroke to Mrs Linton, the Lady of the Grange, wife of a stranger, outcast from what had been my world.

Nelly shakes her head

Shake your head as you will, Nelly. You have helped unsettle me. You should have spoken to Edgar. I'm burning. I wish I was out of doors. I wish I were a girl again, half-savage and hardy and free — laughing at injuries, not maddening under them. Why am I so changed? I should be myself again were I out among the heather on those hills. Open the window wide, quick! Let me get one breath.

Nelly I won't give you your death of cold.

Cathy Won't give me a chance of life, you mean.

Cathy jumps up and opens the window wide. Nelly tries to stop her but Cathy, in her delirium, is strong

Look, I can see the Heights. That's my room with the candle in it. Heathcliff!

Nelly struggles to get Cathy from the window

Nelly (*to Edgar; calling*) Sir! Oh, sir!

Cathy We dared each other to stand on the graves.

Nelly Mr Edgar!

Cathy Soon I'll lie there but they may bury me twelve feet deep and throw the church down over me but I won't rest 'til you are with me!

Edgar enters

Nelly Oh, sir, my poor mistress is ill and she quite masters me!

Edgar Catherine, ill?

*Haggard Cathy stands before Edgar. He is shocked. Cathy wanders
aimlessly*

Nelly She's been fretting here, scarcely eating, never complaining, but
it is nothing.
Edgar Nothing is it, Ellen Dean? You shall account for keeping me
ignorant of this. Shut the window.

Edgar takes Cathy in his arms. Nelly shuts the window

Cathy Are you come, Edgar Linton? You are one of those things that
are ever found when least wanted and when you are wanted, never!
Edgar Cathy.
Cathy I suppose we are to have plenty of lamentations now.
Edgar Catherine, what have you done? Am I nothing to you? Do you
love that wretch, Heath ——
Cathy Hush! Mention that name and I shall spring from the window.
What you touch at present you may have. I don't want you, Edgar. I'm
past wanting you. Return to your books.
Nelly Her mind wanders, sir. She's been talking nonsense the whole
evening. Let her have quiet and proper attendance and she'll rally.
Edgar I want no further advice from you. You knew your mistress's
nature and you encouraged me to ignore her. It was heartless.
Nelly Mrs Linton's nature is headstrong and domineering. Was I to
humour her temper? With Mr Heathcliff? Wink at him and Miss
Isabella? I performed the duty of a faithful servant in telling you and I
have got faithful servants wages! Well, it will teach me to be careful.
Next time you may gather your intelligence for yourself.
Edgar The next time you bring a tale to me you shall quit my service,
Ellen Dean.
Cathy Nelly has played the traitor. She is my hidden enemy. You
witch! You were gathering elf-bolts to hurt us. Let me go and I'll
make her rue, I'll make her howl a recantation! (*She struggles in
Edgar's arms*)

Nelly flees the room

Edgar Cathy, Cathy.

Edgar helps Cathy on to the bed and watches over her

The Lights fade to Black-out

SCENE 2

In the Grange garden at first light

There is a scream. Nelly discovers Mary, a young servant

Mary (*off*) Horrible.

Mary enters. She drags on a dead dog by the rope that has hung it

It's Miss Isabella's dog. Who would do such a thing? And its mistress not here to bury it. She's only gone and run off with Mr Heathcliff.
Edgar (*off*) What's the commotion?
Nelly Say nothing. The master has no heart for a second grief.

Edgar enters

Nelly conceals the dog behind her

Edgar Miss Catherine is sleeping. Is there some news, Nelly?
Nelly No.
Edgar Nothing?
Nelly I'm no teller of tales, sir.
Edgar (*making to leave*) Very well.
Mary Master, our young lady ——
Nelly Hold your noise.
Edgar What ails Isabella?
Mary Heathcliff's run off with her.
Edgar That can't be. No. That's not true.
Mary The lad that fetches milk told me how the blacksmith's lass told him that after midnight they stopped to have a horseshoe fastened in Gimmerton. Anyways, they've run off together. It's all over Gimmerton this morning! Poor dog must've been barking and giving their game away.
Edgar Poor dog?

Nelly reveals the dog. Edgar gags

Nelly Are we to try measures for bringing her back?
Edgar She went of her own accord. Trouble me no more about her. Now she is my sister in name only.

Edgar runs off

Nelly hands the dead dog to Mary

Mary exits with the dog, appalled

Thrushcross Grange

Nelly sits down with Lockwood

Lockwood Mrs Linton?

Nelly Brain fever. No mother could have nursed a child more tenderly than Mr Edgar did her. His health and strength being sacrificed to preserve a mere ruin of humanity.

Lockwood A little harsh.

Nelly In London maybe, not in Yorkshire. I got a letter. (*Taking a letter out of her pocket*) I keep it yet. Any relic of the dead is precious.

Isabella enters

Isabella Dear Ellen, is Mr Heathcliff a man? If so, is he mad? Or is he a devil?

Nelly I thought it a little odd coming from the pen of a bride just out of honeymoon.

Lockwood The beast!

Nelly There are worse men than Heathcliff, Mr Lockwood, I assure you.

Isabella runs to Nelly and embraces her

Isabella Nelly! Have you a letter from Edgar?

Heathcliff enters

Heathcliff If you have anything for Isabella, give it to her. We have no secrets from one another.

Nelly You must not expect a visit or a letter. He wishes you happiness, ma'am.

Isabella Oh.

Heathcliff How is Miss Catherine?

Nelly Mrs Linton will never be what she was but Mr Edgar's duty and humanity will see her cared for.

Heathcliff Do you think I'll leave Catherine to his duty and humanity! I must see her.

Nelly Never through my means. Another encounter between master and you would kill her.

Heathcliff With your aid, that may be avoided.

Nelly Why thrust yourself into her remembrance now when she has forgotten you?

Heathcliff Oh Nelly, you know she has not. Only her words telling me she has forgotten me would ever convince me of that and then I would be in hell. I was a fool to fancy for a moment that she valued Edgar Linton more than me. If he loved her with all the powers of his puny being he couldn't love her as much in eighty years as I could in a day. Catherine has a heart as deep as I have. The sea could be as readily contained in a horse trough as her whole affection be monopolised by him. He is scarcely dearer to her than her dog.

Isabella Catherine and Edgar are as fond of each other as any two people can be.

Heathcliff He's wondrous fond of you too. He's turned you adrift on the world with alacrity.

Isabella He is not aware of what I suffer.

Nelly Somebody's love's come short, in any case. My young lady is looking the worse for her change.

Heathcliff She degenerates into a slut.

Nelly Mrs Heathcliff is accustomed to being looked after.

Heathcliff She abandoned her home under a delusion, picturing me a hero of romance. I can hardly regard her in the light of a rational creature. But at last she begins to know me. I don't perceive the silly smiles and grimaces that provoked me at first. This morning she announced that I had succeeded in making her hate me — a positive labour of Hercules, I assure you! The passion was wholly on one side, I never told her a lie about it. Never in my life have I met with such an abject thing as she is, she even disgraces the name of Linton! I've sometimes relented from pure lack of invention in my experiments on what she could endure and still creep shamefully, cringing back. If she desired to go she might.

Nelly Mr Heathcliff, this is the talk of a madman.

Isabella He's a lying fiend, a monster. I made the attempt to leave before. I dare not repeat it! He has married me, Ellen, only to get power over Edgar. But he shan't get it. I'll die first!

Heathcliff I've a word to say to Ellen in private. (*He grabs Isabella and pushes her forcefully*)

Isabella exits

I must see Catherine. I mean no harm. I only wish to hear from her how she is and why she is ill and if I can be of any use to her. Last night,

I was at the Grange garden for six hours and I'll return tonight. I'll haunt the place. You could let me in unobserved. You'd be preventing mischief.

Nelly My mistress is all nerves. She couldn't bear the surprise.

Heathcliff Am I to fight my way in or will you be my friend? Decide. You'll not leave here 'til you say yes.

He exits

Nelly (*addressing Lockwood*) Well, Mr Lockwood, in the long run he forced me to agreement. I engaged to carry a letter to my mistress. Was I right? Or was I wrong?

Lockwood How did Mrs Linton appear?

Nelly enters Cathy's room. Cathy holds a book but is not reading it. She appears to gaze beyond the room

Nelly She sat in a loose white dress.

Lockwood Loose, you say?

Nelly Her hair falling in tresses about her neck.

Lockwood sighs

An unnatural beauty in her calm. (*Handing Cathy a letter*) There's a letter for you, Mrs Linton. You must read it immediately. Shall I break the seal? (*She does so*) Must I read it, ma'am? It is from Mr Heathcliff.

Cathy starts

He's in the garden and impatient to know what answer I shall bring.

Cathy stands and faces the door

Heathcliff rushes in the room

He takes Cathy in his arms. They kiss

He bestowed more kisses than he ever gave in his life I dare say. But then my mistress started it.

Heathcliff Oh, Cathy. Oh, my life, how can I bear it?

Cathy You and Edgar have broken my heart, Heathcliff! And you both come to bewail the deed to me, as if you were the ones to be pitied. I shall not pity you. You have killed me and thriven on it. How strong you are! How many years do you mean to live after I am gone?

Heathcliff Oh, Cathy.

Cathy (*holding his hair*) I wish I could hold you 'til we were both dead. What care I for your suffering? Why shouldn't you suffer? I do. Will you forget me?

Heathcliff Never, never.

Cathy Will you be happy when I am in the earth? Will you, Heathcliff?

Heathcliff Don't torture me 'til I'm as mad as yourself.

Cathy Will you say twenty years from hence, "That's the grave of Catherine Earnshaw. I loved her long ago and was wretched to lose her, but it is past. I loved many since."

Heathcliff Are you possessed by a devil to talk to me like that when you are dying? All those words will be branded in my memory and eat deeper eternally after you have left me. Catherine, you know I could as soon forget you as my existence. Is it not sufficient for your infernal selfishness that while you are at peace I shall writhe in the torments of hell? (*He moves away from her*)

Cathy I shall not be at peace! Heathcliff, I only wish us never to be parted. Come here and kneel down. You never harmed me in your life. Won't you come here again, do.

Heathcliff doesn't move, he is trying to control his anguish

Oh, you see, Nelly. He would not relent a moment to keep me out of the grave. That is how I am loved.

Heathcliff Don't talk to me of how I love.

Cathy That is not my Heathcliff. I shall love mine yet and take him with me in my soul. I'm tired of being enclosed here. I'm wearying to escape. I wonder he won't come near me. I thought he wished it. Heathcliff, dear! You should not be so sullen now. Do come to me, Heathcliff!

In her eagerness, Cathy rises. Heathcliff turns. Cathy makes a spring and he catches her. They embrace

Nelly Has the mistress fainted?

Heathcliff snarls at Nelly. Nelly backs off. Cathy stirs

Heathcliff Why did you despise me? Why did you betray your own heart, Cathy? I have not one word of comfort. You deserve this. Yes, you may kiss and cry and wring out my kisses and tears, damn you. You loved me. What right did you have to leave me for the poor fancy you felt for Linton? Because misery and degradation and death and nothing that God or Satan could inflict would have parted us — you, of your own will, did it. I have not broken your heart, you have done, and in breaking it you have broken mine. So much the worse for me that I am strong. Do I want to live? Would you like to live with your soul in the grave?

Cathy Let me alone. You left me too! I forgive you — forgive me.

Heathcliff Kiss me again, and don't let me see your eyes. I forgive what you have done to me. I love my murderer, but yours! How can I?

They embrace again

Nelly To a cool spectator they made a strange and fearful picture.

Lockwood (*recoiling*) An unnatural passion!

Nelly (*intervening between Heathcliff and Cathy*) My master will be back shortly.

Heathcliff and Cathy continue to embrace. Heathcliff groans

For heaven's sake, hurry down.

Heathcliff I must go, Cathy. But, if I live, I'll see you again before you sleep. I won't stray five yards from your window.

Cathy You must not go. You shall not.

Heathcliff For one hour.

Cathy Not for a minute.

Nelly You must. Linton will be up immediately.

Cathy No. Oh, don't, don't go. It is the last time. Edgar will not hurt us. Heathcliff I shall die, I shall die.

Heathcliff Hush, hush, my darling.

Nelly Are you going to listen to her ravings? She does not know what she says.

Heathcliff Hush. Catherine, I'll stay.

Nelly Will you ruin her because she has not the wit to help herself? Get up! We are all done for — master, mistress, servant!

Cathy goes limp

Heathcliff Cathy?

Edgar enters

Edgar What is this?

Heathcliff Unless you're a fiend help her first, then speak to me.

Edgar goes over to Cathy and helps her to lie back on the bed

I shall be in the garden, Nelly. I shall visit tomorrow whether Linton be in or not.

Heathcliff exits

Lockwood (*addressing Nelly*) The fury of their embraces, Mrs Dean!
Nelly Far better that she should die than linger a burden and a misery-maker to all about her.

Cathy feels a sudden birth contraction, then gasps and faints

The Lights fade to Black-out

SCENE 4

Thrushcross Grange

The Servants close all the shutters of the house. Edgar is crying at Cathy's death. There is the sound of a baby crying

Nelly comes out of the house, holding a baby. Heathcliff approaches her

Heathcliff She's dead. I've not waited for you to learn that. Don't snivel before me. She wants none of your tears. Give me a true history. How did she die?
Nelly Quietly as a lamb.
Heathcliff Did she say my name?
Nelly Her senses never returned. She lies with a sweet smile on her face. May she wake kindly in the other world.
Heathcliff May she wake in torment! Haunt me, then! Be with me always. Do not leave me in this abyss. I cannot live without my life! I cannot live without my soul!

Heathcliff howls in grief, like a beast, then exits

Nelly He was beyond my skill to console. To the villagers' surprise, Catherine wasn't interned in the chapel but in a corner of the graveyard where the wall is so low that the bilberry plants have climbed over it from the moors and peat mould almost buries it. A simple headstone above.

Lockwood Safest place for her, Mrs Dean.

Nelly You might think so, Mr Lockwood. It wasn't the end of the story.

A storm begins. There is rain and thunder

Nelly sits rocking the baby

> *Isabella runs through the storm, pregnant, wet and scratched by brambles. She arrives at the Grange and makes it to Nelly*

Miss Isabella!

Lockwood More crazed women!

Nelly Upon occasion we are driven to it, Mr Lockwood.

Isabella I have run the whole way from Wuthering Heights, except where I've flown — I've fallen so many times I lost count. Have the goodness to step out and order a carriage to Gimmerton.

Nelly You shall not go tonight.

Isabella I shall, walking or riding. I have to get away.

Nelly I'll stir nowhere, young lady, 'til you have put on dry things and had some tea.

Isabella (*taking off her wedding ring*) This is the last thing of his I have about me. Give me the poker. (*Grabbing the poker*) I'll smash it. (*She lays the ring down and smashes the poker on it*)

Nelly Your wedding ring!

Isabella Incarnate devil. He'll have to buy me another if he can find me. Catherine had perverted taste to esteem Heathcliff so dearly. Monster! He should be blotted out of creation. (*She laughs*)

Nelly Give over laughing, miss. It's sadly out of place here and you in your condition. What has driven you to flight at last?

Isabella Put poor Cathy's baby away. I don't like to see it. We parted unreconciled, remember.

Nelly puts the baby down

Yester-evening I sat in my nook reading 'til late. It seemed dismal to go upstairs. I kept thinking of Cathy in her new-made grave.

The kitchen scene at Wuthering Heights appears

> *Isabella enters the scene, followed by Hindley who sits and drinks*

The latch rattles

Hindley I fastened the latch. I'll keep him out five minutes. You object?

Isabella You may keep him out all night for me.

Hindley You and I have a great debt to settle with that man out yonder. Mrs Heathcliff, I'll ask you nothing but to sit still and be dumb. He'll be our death unless we overreach him.

Heathcliff knocks on the door

Damn the hellish villain. He knocks at the door as if he were master here already. (*He draws out a pistol*)

Isabella (*to Nelly*) I surveyed the weapon — a hideous notion struck me. How powerful I should be, possessing such an instrument.

Hindley Promise to hold your tongue and you'll be a free woman.

Isabella No, I'll not hold my tongue. Violence wounds those who resort to it worse than their enemies.

Hindley Am I to lose all? Is Hareton to be a beggar? I will have my money back he's cheated me of and hell shall have his black soul. (*He draws out a knife*) I'll do you a kindness in spite of yourself, and Hareton justice.

Heathcliff knocks on the door again, then moves to the window. Isabella has no choice but to shout out

Isabella You better seek shelter elsewhere tonight. Mr Earnshaw has a mind to shoot you!

Heathcliff (*off*) Open the door or I'll make you repent.

Isabella I cannot commit murder, however tempting. Hindley stands sentinel with a knife and pistol.

Hindley You love the villain yet – you base coward.

Heathcliff (*off*) Let me in by the kitchen door then, hussy!

Heathcliff runs to the outer kitchen door and smashes it in

Hindley runs out

A shot is fired

Heathcliff and Hindley enter

Isabella Ellen, don't judge me as wicked, but I was fearfully disappointed he wasn't dead!

Heathcliff kicks Hindley and beats his head against the flags

Joseph enters

There is the sound of dogs barking

Joseph Soa, yah been murthering on him? If iver I seed a seeght loike this! Whet is thur tuh do, nah.
Heathcliff Clean him up. (*To Isabella*) And you conspired with him against me, viper!
Isabella If I were you, I'd go and stretch myself over Catherine's grave and die like a faithful dog! Pray to your black father all you want, it won't bring her back!

Hindely comes round with a groan and Isabella tends to him

Heathcliff Get up and be gone out of my sight.
Isabella I loved Catherine too and her brother requires attendance, which for her sake I shall supply.
Heathcliff Get up, you wretched idiot, before I stamp you to death.
Isabella If poor Catherine had assumed the contemptible, degrading title of Mrs Heathcliff she wouldn't have borne your behaviour quietly. Her detestation and disgust would have found a voice! She would have grown to hate you like I do.

Heathcliff rushes towards Isabella and is stopped by Hindley

(*Making to leave*) I enraged him and that pleasure awoke my instinct for self-preservation so I broke free! I dare not stay. Goodbye, Nelly. I'll write to you. You must keep my whereabouts a secret, mind.

Isabella exits

Nelly Her new abode was South London. Her son was born and named Linton, an ailing, peevish creature from the start. Fortunately, its mother died before she saw Heathcliff claim it.
Lockwood A sad end to a bewitching creature. One wishes she'd found someone honourable, passionate and dashing. Unfortunately, we're thin on the ground.
Nelly Poor Hindley drunk himself to death, dying in debt to Mr Heathcliff for the whole of the Heights. The guest was now the master.
Lockwood And young Cathy?
Nelly Grew like a larch.

SCENE 5

Young Cathy enters and looks out over the moors

Nelly A real beauty in the face.
Lockwood A man might be in some danger there if he had not the sense
to be cautious.
Nelly Her only flaw; a propensity to be saucy.
Lockwood Saucy, eh?
Young Cathy Only a little further, Ellen.
Nelly We have strayed too far from the Grange Park, Miss Cathy.
Young Cathy But I know the park and I don't know the moors. I'm
sixteen now, Nelly, I think I might be allowed some freedom. I see
a nest!

Heathcliff appears unnoticed. Hareton waits behind Heathcliff

Young Cathy finds a nest and Heathcliff surprises her

Heathcliff Poacher! These are my grouse.
Young Cathy I don't mean to take them. I just wished to see the eggs.
Papa told me there were quantities here.
Heathcliff Papa?
Young Cathy Mr Linton of the Grange. I thought you didn't know me
or you wouldn't have spoken to me like that.
Heathcliff So you are Catherine Linton?
Young Cathy Yes. Why do you stare like that? Who are you? (*She
points to Hareton*) Is he your son?
Heathcliff No. But I have one and you should meet him.
Nelly On no account, Miss Cathy.
Young Cathy Why? I can't just be satisfied with your company and
Papa's my whole life.
Heathcliff (*indicating Hareton*) He'll escort you to fetch my son. My
house is just by.

Hareton and Young Cathy exit

Nelly is held back by Heathcliff

Nelly Mr Heathcliff, it's very wrong. You know you mean no good.
Miss Catherine is forbidden by her father to visit the Heights.
Heathcliff We can persuade her to keep the visit secret. Where's the
harm of it? She must meet my son sometime. My design is as honest

as possible; that the two cousins will fall in love and get married. I'm
acting generously to your master. His young chit has no expectations
and she'll be provided for as joint successor with Linton.

Nelly You mean to have her property. Over my dead body.

Heathcliff Let's hope it won't come to that.

Young Cathy enters Wuthering Heights with Linton

Young Cathy Nelly! This is my cousin, Linton Heathcliff! (*To
Heathcliff*) You are my uncle, then. I thought I liked you. Why don't
you visit the Grange with Linton? You are such close neighbours, it's
very odd. I'll take this walk every morning.

Nelly Miss Cathy ——

Young Cathy And you won't stop me, Ellen.

Heathcliff I better tell you, Edgar Linton has a prejudice against me.
We quarrelled at one time in our lives and if you mention your visits
here, he'll veto them.

Young Cathy But Linton and I have no quarrel. He must come to the
Grange then.

Linton It would be too far. Four miles would kill me. No, you come
here, Miss Catherine, once a week.

Nelly It's against your father's wishes, miss.

Hareton enters. He speaks with a broad Yorkshire accent

Heathcliff (*to Hareton*) Have you been preening yourself? Stuck your
head under a tap?

Hareton blushes

Is he not a handsome lad?

Cathy pulls a face. Heathcliff laughs

Have you not a weasels' or a rabbits' nest to show your cousin?

Linton I'd rather sit inside by the fire.

Heathcliff Hareton, show her round the place since Linton is off
colour.

Young Cathy No thank you. You may tell me what's that above the
front door back there?

Hareton Some damnable writing. I cannot read it.

Young Cathy Can't read it! It's English. I want to know why it's
there.

Linton He doesn't know his letters. Can you believe in the existence of such a colossal dunce?

Young Cathy Is he simple? He looks so stupid, when I ask him questions I'm not sure he understands me. I can hardly understand him, I'm sure.

Nelly Hareton's your cousin, Miss Cathy.

Young Cathy That brute?

Linton There's nothing the matter but laziness is there, Earnshaw? The consequence of scorning "book larning", as you would say.

Hareton Why, where the devil is the use on't?

Linton Where is the use of the devil in that sentence? Papa told you not to use any bad words and you can't open your mouth without one! Do try to behave like a gentleman, now do. Have you noticed, Catherine, his frightful Yorkshire pronunciation?

Young Cathy laughs

Hareton (*to Young Cathy*) Damn your mucky pride! I'll go t'hell before I'll look sideways at ye again. (*To Linton*) If thou weren't more a lass than a lad I'd fell thee this minute. I would. Pitiful lath of a crater!

Hareton runs off

Linton So I'm a crater now. The joke is the inscription reads his name, "Hareton Earnshaw". Some clodhopping old ancestor of his!

Cathy and Linton laugh and whisper together. Heathcliff smiles

Heathcliff (*to Nelly*) Hareton has satisfied my expectations. If he was born a fool I should not enjoy it half so much. I can sympathize with all his feelings, having suffered them myself. I've got him faster than his scoundrel father secured me. And lower. One tree will grow as crooked as another with the same wind to twist it.

Nelly You've cast him out like a fledgling dimmock! Cathy, leave your spiteful sayings. Come home now.

Young Cathy kisses Linton goodbye

Linton Come soon.

Young Cathy Tomorrow. I won't fail you.

Heathcliff and Linton exit

I didn't think of loving him at first. It just happened.

Nelly Loving! Did anybody hear the like? You've hardly been with him an hour in your life! We'll see what your father says to such loving. It'll grieve him and he's not well. He'd tell you, Heathcliff is a wicked man.

Young Cathy But Linton is expecting me. I'll explain to father.

Nelly You say a word of this to your father and I'll get my notice. Do you hear, young lady? Not a word.

Young Cathy That's lying, Nelly.

Nelly Do you want me sent away?

Young Cathy Poor Linton. (*She sighs*)

They exit

The Lights cross fade

SCENE 6

On the moors

Lockwood A solitary tear on the cheek enhances a woman.

Nelly You're very lively and interested when I talk about Miss Cathy.

Lockwood Stop, my good friend. I am of the busy world and to its arms I must one day return. Why should I venture my tranquility?

Nelly No one can see Catherine Linton and not love her.

Lockwood But I've sworn to break no more hearts! I'm an absolute danger to the female sex, Mrs Dean.

Nelly Don't worry yourself on that account, Mr Lockwood.

Nelly joins Young Cathy outdoors

Young Cathy The last of the bluebells. I'll not touch it. It looks melancholy, doesn't it, Ellen?

Nelly Yes, about as starved and sackless as you. Your cheeks are bloodless. You're so low. Let's hold hands and run.

Young Cathy No. (*She wipes a tear*)

Nelly You mustn't cry because Papa has a cold. Be thankful it's nothing worse.

Young Cathy It is something worse. What shall I do when Papa leaves me?

Nelly Pick that bluebell and we'll take it to him.

Young Cathy gets the flower

Heathcliff enters, carrying a riding whip

Heathcliff Ho, Miss Linton. I had heard you often walk this way of a morning. I want an explanation from you.

Young Cathy I shan't speak to you, Mr Heathcliff.

Heathcliff It's concerning my son. Yes. You have cause to blush. You wearied of him, did you? Well, Linton was in earnest. He was in love and as true as I live he's dying for you.

Young Cathy Dying?

Heathcliff Breaking his heart at your fickleness. He gets worse daily and will be under the sod before summer unless you restore him.

Nelly Don't believe his vile nonsense. How can a person die for love of a stranger?

Heathcliff I like you, Mrs Dean, but I don't like your double-dealing. (*To Young Cathy*) My bonny lass, I swear on my salvation, he's going to his grave and none but you can save him.

Nelly Come home, Cathy.

Heathcliff Linton is dying. Grief and disappointment are hastening his death. A word from you would be his best medicine. He dreams of you day and night. He cannot be persuaded that you don't hate him!

Young Cathy I must tell Linton it is not my fault.

Nelly, Heathcliff and Young Cathy exit

The Lights fade to Black-out

SCENE 7

At Wuthering Heights

Linton rests on a couch

Young Cathy Well, Linton, are you glad to see me?

Linton Don't kiss me, it takes my breath. Why didn't you come to visit me? Papa swore it was owing to me. He said I was a pitiful, shuffling, worthless thing and you despised me. Do you, miss?

Young Cathy I wish you'd call me Cathy. I don't despise you. Next to Papa and Ellen, I love you better than anyone.

Linton has a fit of coughing

How ill you look.

Linton (*panting*) No, better, better.

Young Cathy You are thinner.

Linton I'm tired and often sick in the mornings. Papa says I grow too fast.

Young Cathy I can't stay, Linton. My father is sick. I don't like to be long from his bedside.

Linton No, I beg you, stay. Catherine, if my father asks you about me don't lead him to suppose I've been silent and stupid. Don't look downcast as you are doing now for you'll provoke him against me and he is very hard. Leave me and I shall be killed. My life is in your hands. Kind, good, sweet Catherine, perhaps you will consent.

Young Cathy Consent to what?

Linton grabs Cathy. He kisses her hands

Nelly and Heathcliff enter. Heathcliff locks the door. Nelly starts

Heathcliff You shall have tea before you go home. The servants are off and though I am used to being alone I'd rather have some interesting company. Miss Linton, take your seat by him. I'll give you what I have — it's hardly worth accepting but I have nothing else to offer. It is Linton, I mean. How she does stare at me. It is odd what a savage feeling I have to anything that is afraid of me. Had I been born where laws are less strict and tastes less dainty, I should treat myself to a slow vivisection of those two as an evening's amusement. By hell I hate the two of them.

Young Cathy I am not afraid of you. Give me that key or … I will have it. I wouldn't eat or drink here if I were starving! (*She snatches at the key*)

Heathcliff Stand off, Catherine Linton, or I shall knock you down and that will make Mrs Dean mad.

Young Cathy does not stand off. She catches Heathcliff's hand

Young Cathy We will go.

Young Cathy bites Heathcliff's hand. He frees it and then slaps both sides of her face

Nelly You villain!

Young Cathy rushes at Heathcliff. He pushes her aside and she staggers back. Young Cathy is stunned

Heathcliff I know how to chastise children, you see.

Young Cathy runs to Nelly, who comforts her

Nelly Master Linton. You know what your diabolical father is after. Tell us or I shall box your ears.
Young Cathy Yes, Linton, you must tell.
Heathcliff Tell them.
Linton *(to Nelly)* Give me some water, I'm thirsty.

Nelly hands him a cup of water

Mrs Dean, go away. I don't like you standing over me like that. Don't cry, Cathy, your tears will fall in my cup. Papa wants us to be married. And he's afraid of me dying if we wait so we are to be married in the morning and you are to stay here all night.
Nelly Marry you? My beautiful, healthy, hearty girl — tie herself to such a little, perishing monkey? You want whipping for bringing us here with your dastardly puling tricks!
Young Cathy *(running to the locked door)* Ellen, I'll burn that door down but I'll get out.
Heathcliff Linton, have done and get to bed. By chance you have managed tolerably. I'll look to the rest.

Linton exits

Young Cathy Mr Heathcliff, let me go home. Papa will be miserable if I stay. What would he think if I am gone the whole night? I promise to marry Linton willingly, why should you force me?
Nelly Let him dare force you, there is a law in the land.
Heathcliff Miss Linton, I shall enjoy myself remarkably in thinking your father will be miserable. You couldn't have hit on a surer way of fixing your residence under my roof for the next twenty-four hours!
Young Cathy Send Ellen then, to know that I am safe! Or marry me now. Poor Papa. What will he think?
Heathcliff That you are tired of waiting on him and run off for a little amusement.
Young Cathy Mr Heathcliff, you're a cruel man but you're not a fiend. Have you never loved anybody in your life, Uncle? Don't turn away, do look!

Young Cathy grabs Heathcliff pleadingly. He shakes her off

Nelly She has her mother's eyes, has she not?

Heathcliff registers this with shock

Heathcliff Get your lizard fingers off me. I'd rather be hugged by a snake. How the devil can you dream of fawning on me? I detest you!

Heathcliff exits

Young Cathy frantically tries to find a way out

Nelly We passed a dismal night and then ...

Heathcliff opens the door

Heathcliff Come here.

Heathcliff grabs Young Cathy and pulls her out

Nelly You'll not take her.

Heathcliff pushes Nelly back in

Heathcliff and Young Cathy exit

(*Sinking to the floor*) Oh, Mr Lockwood! I shed some bitter tears that night. How had I let this come to pass? Locked away for two nights — my thoughts brewed. I passed harsh judgement on myself and my many derelicitions of duty from which it struck me that all the misfortunes of my employers sprang. In my imagination I thought Heathcliff less guilty than I!

The Lights cross fade

SCENE 8

Wuthering Heights. Morning

Zillah enters with shawl and a basket over her arm

Nelly Zillah!
Zillah Mrs Dean! Well, there is talk about you at Gimmerton. I never thought, but you were sunk in the Blackhorse Marsh and missy with you, 'til master told me you'd been found and he'd lodged you here!
Nelly What a tale! Your master is a true scoundrel. He shall answer for it!

Zillah It's not his tale — they all say that in the village. The master sent me up just now to bid you go to the Grange. He wouldn't let you out before 'cause he said the bog water had got into your head and you weren't in your senses. You'll be in time for the squire's funeral.

Nelly Mr Edgar is not dead?

Zillah No, not yet. Dr Kenneth thinks he might last another day.

Zillah exits

Linton enters, sucking a lollipop

Linton Morning.

Nelly (*grabbing Linton*) Where is Miss Catherine? Is she gone?

Linton She's upstairs. We won't let her out.

Nelly Won't let her? You little idiot. Direct me to her room immediately or I'll make you sing out sharply.

Linton Papa would make you sing out if you got her. He's says I'm not to be soft with Catherine. She's my wife and it's shameful that she should wish to leave me. He says she hates me and wants me to die because she wants all my money but she shan't have it and she shan't go home.

Nelly Have you forgotten all Catherine's kindnesses to you! That's fine gratitude. You heartless, selfish boy!

Linton She cries so I can't bear it. I can't sleep. Father threatened to strangle her once if she wouldn't shut up so she did but then she started again the instant he left the room.

Nelly Is Mr Heathcliff gone out?

Linton He's in the court. I am to be master of the Grange when uncle dies and Catherine always spoke of it as her house. It isn't hers, it's mine. Papa says everything she has is mine. All her nice books and her pretty birds and her pony, Minny. She offered to give them to me if I would give her the key to let her out but I told her she had nothing to give — they were all, all mine.

Nelly And you can get the key if you choose.

Linton Yes.

Nelly Which is her apartment?

Linton I shan't tell you.

Nelly pinches him

Ow. It's the secret room with panelling down the narrow stairs to the small corridor, second on the left.

Nelly pushes Linton off

Linton exits

Nelly She saw her father one last time, Mr Lockwood. Then she was taken off to live with her new husband. Her property was his. And when he died shortly after it all went to Heathcliff.

Lockwood If ever a girl needed rescuing, Mrs Dean.

Nelly Don't get too excited Mr Lockwood, you'll knock over your night pot.

Lockwood Wise words, Mrs Dean. Do you still feel the fault for all that lay at your door?

Nelly No. That was in my imagination. Not reality. That's it, Mr Lockwood. That's everything.

Nelly exits

The Lights cross fade

SCENE 9

Lockwood is alone on stage

Lockwood But it wasn't to be the last I was to learn of this curious history. I recovered rapidly and returned to London. I can't say I missed these bleak northern skies. Or the dreary physiognomy of its people! But fate would draw me back. Or perhaps it was young Mrs Heathcliff's bewitching ... eyes. Come September I was invited to devastate the moors of a friend in the north. (*He aims taking a shot at a grouse and mimics firing*) Yes! On my way home I found myself unexpectedly within fifteen miles of Gimmerton. I decided to visit the Heights.

A new scene at Wuthering Heights opens before Lockwood. It is late summer and birds are singing

Young Cathy and Hareton are seated together, reading a book

Young Cathy Con-trary. That for the third time, you dunce! I'm not going to tell you again. Recollect or I'll pull your hair.

Hareton Contrary then. And now, kiss me for minding so well.

Young Cathy No, read it over first correctly without a single mistake.

Hareton (*reading*) "Contrary to her first opinion, she decided she liked him very well indeed."

Young Cathy laughs, Hareton kisses her

Nelly appears at the doorway, singing and sewing

Joseph pokes his head out of a window and waves his bible

Joseph It's a blazing shame ut aw cannot open t'blessed book but yah set up them glories to Sattan un' all t'flaysome wickedness ut iver wer born intuh t'warld.

Nelly No, we should be sitting in flaming faggots, I suppose. Read your bible. This is Fairy Anne's wedding, a bonny tune. It goes with a dance. (*She does a few steps*)

Joseph Oh, yah're a raight nowt; un shoo's another, un that poor lad 'ull be last atween ye. Poor lad, he's witched. Aw'm certain on it. Oh Lord, judge 'em!

Joseph pokes his head back in

Lockwood Mrs Dean?

Nelly Why bless me, it's Mr Lockwood. How should you think of returning all this way? All's shut up at the Grange. You should have given us notice.

Lockwood I depart again tomorrow. I came to finish my business with —— (*He glances at Cathy*)

Cathy and Hareton exit

Your master.

Nelly What business, sir?

Lockwood About the ... rent.

Nelly Oh, then it is with Mrs Heathcliff you must settle. (*She pauses*) Ah, you have not heard of Heathcliff's death I see.

Lockwood Heathcliff, dead?

Nelly Three months since. He had a queer end.

Heathcliff appears in the kitchen

I was summonsed back to the Heights two weeks after your leaving us and I accepted. Joyfully for Miss Catherine's sake.

Young Cathy and Hareton come through the door, laughing. Joseph follows

Joseph Maister. Aw cannot stand it.

Heathcliff What, you idiot?

Joseph It's yon flaysome, graceless quean, ut's witched arh lad, wi her bold een, un her forrard ways — 'til — nay t'fair brusts my heart. He's forgetten all 'e done for him, 'un made on him, un'goan riven up a whole row ut t'grandest blackberry brambles in t'garden.

Heathcliff Is the fool drunk? Hareton, is it you he's finding fault with?

Hareton I've pulled up two or three bushes.

Heathcliff Why have you pulled them up?

Young Cathy We wanted to plant some flowers there. I'm the person to blame. I wished him to do it.

Heathcliff Who the devil gave you leave to touch a stick about the place? (*To Hareton*) And who ordered you to obey her?

Young Cathy You shouldn't grudge me a few yards of earth when you have taken all my land.

Heathcliff Your land? Insolent slut. You never had any.

Young Cathy And my money!

Heathcliff Silence! Get gone.

Young Cathy And Hareton's land and his money. Hareton and I are friends now.

Heathcliff Friends? How? Lad?

Hareton We are ... friends.

Young Cathy I'm teaching him to read! He likes books.

Heathcliff Books!

Young Cathy Yes, why shouldn't he read? I like to teach him and I'm sorry for the way I treated him before.

Heathcliff Can you read now?

Hareton Tolerably.

Heathcliff (*to Young Cathy*) You hussy!

Heathcliff gets up and begins pursuing Young Cathy about the table

Young Cathy If you strike me Hareton will strike you, so you may as well sit down.

Heathcliff If Hareton does not turn you out of the room, I'll strike him to hell, damnable witch! Dare you pretend to rouse him against me? I'll kill her.

Hareton Cathy ...

Young Cathy He'll not obey you any more, wicked man.

Hareton comes between them

Hareton (*to Young Cathy*) Whisht — I'll not hear you speak to him so, Cathy, have done.

Young Cathy You won't let him strike me?

Heathcliff I'll thrash the living daylights out of you!
Hareton (*beckoning Young Cathy out with him*) Come then.
Heathcliff (*grabbing Young Cathy's hair*) Too late. Accursed witch.
Hareton Don't hurt her. Let her go this once.

Hareton tries to disengage them. Heathcliff brings Cathy's face up. Seeing her eyes he freezes and suddenly lets go

Heathcliff Your eyes ... are your mother's. Leave me. All of you.

Young Cathy and Hareton exit

Heathcliff is alone. He appears agitated and strange

The Lights fade to black-out

SCENE 10

Wuthering Heights. Night-time

Heathcliff stands in the shadows, staring out of a window. Nelly approaches him, bearing a candle

Nelly You've kept alone these last days, sir.
Heathcliff Nelly, there is a strange change approaching.
Nelly What do you mean, Mr Heathcliff? You have no feeling of illness?
Heathcliff No. I'm dying.
Nelly Dying? Aren't you afraid of death?
Heathcliff Afraid? No. The day Cathy was buried I went to the churchyard.

The atmosphere of the churchyard appears. It is dark, the wind moans and trees creak

I got a spade from the toolhouse and began to delve with all my might. It scraped the coffin. I fell to work with my hands. I'd have her in my arms again!
Nelly You were very wicked, Mr Heathcliff, to disturb the dead.

Heathcliff is in the moment, imagining the grave before him and kneeling by it

Heathcliff The wood commenced cracking about the screws. I was on the point of attaining my object when I heard a sigh from someone close at the edge of the grave. There was another sigh, close to my ear — warm breath — I knew no living thing was by. I felt that Cathy was there, not under me, but on the earth. Relief flowed through my heart. I was unspeakably consoled. Her presence was with me. I re-filled her grave. You may laugh, but I was sure it was she. I have a strong faith in ghosts. She has disturbed me night and day through eighteen years, incessantly, remorselessly. It has been a strange way of killing, not by inches, but by fractions of hair breadths to beguile me with the spectre of hope all those years! When I slept in her chamber, the moment I closed my eyes she was either outside the window or resting her darling head on the same pillow as she did as a child. I must open my lids to see — to be always disappointed. Until last night. (*He stands and makes to leave*)

Nelly Where are you going, sir? I don't think it is right to wander out of doors in this moist season. You were out last night, too. Where were you?

Heathcliff Until last night I was on the threshold of hell. Today I am within sight of my heaven. I have my eyes on it — hardly three feet sever me. And now you better go. You'll neither see nor hear anything to frighten you if you refrain from prying.

Nelly Prying? (*She holds the candle to Heathcliff's face, giving an eerie and sinister effect; to Lockwood*) Oh, Mr Lockwood! His face was ghastly as a ghoul or a vampire. Where did he come from — the little dark thing harboured by a good man to his bane? (*To Heathcliff*) Mr Heathcliff, Master! Don't for God's sake stare so.

Heathcliff When day breaks, send for Green the attorney. I have not written my will.

Nelly Don't talk so, Mr Heathcliff. You need some food and repose. You're a person starving.

Heathcliff I cannot eat or rest. My soul's bliss kills my body. I'm too happy but not yet happy enough.

Nelly Strange happiness! You have lived a selfish, unchristian life and you will be unfit for heaven unless you make a change before you die.

Heathcliff I don't wish to be fit for your heaven, Nelly. I do not want it. I don't covet it. I don't value it.

Nelly A sin to say so.

Heathcliff All I ever loved is of this earth. My heaven is here. When I die no minister need come, nor need anything be said over me.

Nelly If they refuse to bury you in the churchyard because you have willed your death?

Heathcliff Then you must have me removed there secretly and placed beside Cathy, so that our flesh may dissolve together. Do it or I shall prove to you practically that the dead are not annihilated. I know you'll see that done because you know I speak truth.
Nelly No!
Heathcliff Get gone, Mrs Dean!

The night becomes ferocious. There is wind and rain

Cathy, do come. Oh my heart's darling, hear me this time!
Nelly Ah!

Nelly flees

There is the sound of dogs howling as trees groan and beat against the windows. There is darkness and lightning

Heathcliff Cathy at last!

Nelly and Servants enter and run about, trying to close windows which are opened again, banging with increased ferocity

Nelly discovers Heathcliff dead. She screams

Joseph hurries in

Joseph Th' divil's harried off his soul. And he mun hev his carcass intuh bargain for owt I care. Ech. What a wicked un he looks girnning at death. (*He does a caper*)

Hareton runs in

Joseph stops and gets on his knees

Oh Lord, have mercy on us sinners.

Hareton gets to his knees in sorrow

Cathy runs in and goes to Nelly. They stand for a moment

The Lights fade to Black-out

SCENE 11

Nelly He was buried as promised. Beside Catherine. I saw to that.

Lockwood That's the true end of your tale, Mrs Dean.

Nelly Country folks swear on their bible that he walks. Near the church, on the moor. Joseph says he's seen the two on 'em from his chamber window, every rainy night since his death.

Lockwood The old man's a fool.

Nelly About a month ago I met a young lad, just at the turn of the Heights. It was a dark evening, threatening thunder.

A Lad appears

He was crying terribly. I thought maybe his lambs were skittish and would not be guided.

Nelly (*to the Lad*) What's the matter, my little man?

Lad There's Heathcliff and a woman yonder, under t'nab, un aw darnut pass 'em.

Nelly I see nothing.

Lad I won't go on.

Nelly Take the road lower down, lad.

The Lad runs off

Lockwood Country superstition. The natives here are simpler than those in the city, I've observed.

Nelly You'll have noticed love in the air then.

Lockwood What?

Nelly They are to be married on New Year's Eve.

Lockwood Married?

Nelly Yes, and we shall be glad when we shift to the Grange.

Hareton and Young Cathy can be seen together holding hands and walking into the house

(*Indicating Hareton and Young Cathy*) They are afraid of nothing. Together they'd brave Satan and all his legions.

Lockwood There was a time when I thought your young mistress was rather partial to me.

Nelly In your dreams, Mr Lockwood.

Lockwood Mrs Dean. Here. (*He gives her some money*) Thank you for a diverting tale.

Nelly It is my life, sir, I don't ask money for it.

Nelly stalks off and closes the door behind her, leaving Lockwood by himself

Lockwood I passed by the Heights on my walk home. (*He sees the house*) When beneath its walls I perceived decay had made progress, even in seven months. Many a window showed black gaps deprived of glass, slates jutted off here and there, to be worked off in coming autumn storms. I sought and discovered the three headstones in the graveyard next to the moor. I lingered round them. Under this benign sky, with the moths fluttering among the heath and harebells and listening to the soft wind breathing through the grass, I wonder how anyone could ever imagine unquiet slumbers for the sleepers in that quiet earth. (*He smiles and makes to leave*)

A wind whips up suddenly. The sky darkens and rain begins to fall

Nelly appears and watches Lockwood

Lockwood hears an eerie sound. It is of children laughing and playing, but it is ghostly. He senses something but does not see anyone

He hurries off

Cathy and Heathcliff enter, stand and raise their arms to the heavens as if raising the dead

Darkness

FURNITURE AND PROPERTY LIST

ACT I
SCENE 1

On stage:	Table. *On it*: tray containing tea things
	Chairs
	Fireplace
	Cupboards
	High, stocked bookshelf
	Window and shutters
Off stage:	Pitchfork (**Hareton**)
	Lantern (**Joseph**)
	Bucket of cold water (**Zillah**)
Personal:	**Lockwood**: Guide book

SCENE 2

On stage:	Bed
	Window and shutters
	Bookshelf and books
	Lighted candle for **Zillah**
Off stage:	Staves (**Crowd**)

SCENE 3

On stage:	Chair, blanket, handkerchief (**Lockwood**)
Off stage:	Breakfast (**Nelly**)

SCENE 4

On stage:	Wuthering Heights. As before

SCENE 5

On stage:	Wuthering Heights. As before
	Lantern, candle, matches (**Nelly**)
Off stage:	Lantern, stone (**Heathcliff**)

SCENE 6

On stage: Wuthering Heights. As before

SCENE 7

On stage: Wuthering Heights. As before
                Pot of apple sauce, cloth, brush (**Nelly**)

SCENE 8

On stage: Wuthering Heights. As before
                Plate of food for **Heathcliff**

Off stage: Baby, bottle (**Hindley**)

SCENE 9

Set: Almanac on wall
                Duster for **Nelly**
                Something to put the baby in
                Brandy for **Hareton**

Off stage: Knife (**Hindley**)

SCENE 10

On stage: Bench

SCENE 11

On stage: Tea things and chairs for **Cathy** and **Edgar**
                Table

SCENE 12

No props required

SCENE 13

On stage: Thrushcross Grange
                Water

ACT II
SCENE 1

On stage: Window
                Bed and pillow

Off stage: Bowl of gruel, spoon (**Nelly**)

SCENE 2

On stage: Garden

Off stage: Dead dog on a rope (**Mary**)

SCENE 3

Off stage: Book for **Cathy**

Personal: **Nelly**: two letters, one in an envelope

SCENE 4

On stage: Thrushcross Grange
                 Poker

Off stage: Baby (**Nelly**)

Personal: **Hindley**: pistol, knife
                 Isabella: wedding ring

SCENE 5

On stage: Nest (**Young Cathy**)

SCENE 6

Off stage: Riding whip (**Heathcliff**)

SCENE 7

On stage: Wuthering Heights. As before
                 Couch

Off stage: Key (**Heathcliff**)
                 Cup of water (**Nelly**)

SCENE 8

On stage: Wuthering Heights. As before

Off stage: Shawl, basket (**Zillah**)
                 Lollipop (**Linton**)

SCENE 9

On stage: Table

Off stage: Book (**Young Cathy** and **Hareton**)
                Sewing things (**Nelly**)
                Bible (**Joseph**)

SCENE 10

On stage: Wuthering Heights. As before

Off stage: Candle (**Nelly**)

SCENE 11

Personal: **Lockwood**: money

LIGHTING PLOT

ACT I, Scene 1

To open: Evening

No cues

ACT I, Scene 2

Cue 1	**Heathcliff**: "Hear me this time, Catherine, at last!" *Fade to Black-out*	(Page 9)

ACT I, Scene 3

To open: Exterior light, daytime

Cue 2	**Nelly**: "He brought a wife." *Fade to Black-out*	(Page 12)

ACT I, Scene 4

To open: Interior light, daytime

Cue 3	**Cathy** pulls **Heathcliff** away and off they run *Fade to Black-out*	(Page 13)

ACT I, Scene 5

To open: Darkness

Cue 4	**Nelly** enters with a lantern *Increase light*	(Page 13)
Cue 5	**Heathcliff** and **Cathy** enter the house *Interior light*	(Page 14)
Cue 6	**Nelly** pushes **Heathcliff** along to retire *Fade to Black-out*	(Page 17)

ACT I, Scene 6

To open: Interior light, daytime

Cue 14   **Cathy**: "Heathcliff! My heart will break."   (Page 38)
                Fade to Black-out

ACT II, Scene 1

To open: Exterior light, morning

Cue 15   **Nelly** joins **Cathy** in her room   (Page 39)
                Interior light

Cue 16   **Edgar** helps **Cathy** onto the bed and watches over her   (Page 42)
                Fade to Black-out

ACT II, Scene 2

To open: First light

ACT II, Scene 3

Cue 17   **Cathy** gasps and faints   (Page 49)
                Fade to Black-out

ACT II, Scene 4

To open: Interior light

ACT II, Scene 5

Cue 18   **Nelly** and **Young Cathy** exit   (Page 56)
                Cross fade

ACT II, Scene 6

Cue 19   **Nelly**, **Heathcliff** and **Young Cathy** exit   (Page 57)
                Fade to Black-out

ACT II, Scene 7

To open: Interior light

Cue 20   **Nelly**: " ... Heathcliff less guilty than I."   (Page 60)
                Cross fade

ACT II, Scene 8

Cue 21   **Nelly** exits   (Page 62)
                Cross fade

ACT II, Scene 9

| *Cue* 22 | **Lockwood**: "I decided to visit the Heights."
 Interior light, late summer | (Page 62) |

| *Cue* 23 | **Young Cathy** and **Hareton** exit. **Heathcliff** is alone
 Fade to Black-out | (Page 65) |

ACT II, Scene 10

To open: Night-time

| *Cue* 24 | **Heathcliff**: " ... was buried I went to the churchyard."
 Atmosphere of a churchyard; darkness | (Page 65) |

| *Cue* 25 | Trees groan and beat against the windows
 Darkness and lightning | (Page 67) |

| *Cue* 26 | **Young Cathy** runs to **Nelly**. They stand for a moment
 Fade to Black-out | (Page 67) |

ACT II, Scene 11

To open: Daylight

| *Cue* 27 | **Lockwood** smiles and makes to leave
 Sky darkens | (Page 69) |

| *Cue* 27 | **Cathy** and **Heathcliff** raise their arms to the heavens
 Darkness | (Page 69) |

EFFECTS PLOT

ACT I

Cue 1   **Lockwood** knocks on the door   (Page 1)
Dogs barking

Cue 2   **Lockwood**: "I'm Mr Lockwood, his new tenant."   (Page 1)
Dogs barking

Cue 3   **Joseph** bangs the window shut   (Page 1)
Dogs barking

Cue 4   **Joseph** slams the window shut   (Page 2)
Wind howls and snow begins to fall

Cue 5   **Lockwood** sits   (Page 2)
Dog snarls

Cue 6   **Lockwood** pets Juno uncertainly   (Page 3)
Dog snaps at **Lockwood**

Cue 7   **Joseph**: "May the Lord deliver us from evil!"   (Page 3)
Snow blows in; dogs howl

Cue 8   **Joseph**: "Maister, he's staling t'lantern, maister!"   (Page 5)
Dogs barking

Cue 9   **Crowd, Branderham** and **Joseph** exit   (Page 7)
*Tree branch taps against window; wind wuthers; the
  tapping is insistent*

Cue 10   To open Scene 5   (Page 13)
Wind and rain

Cue 11   **Heathcliff**: "Flee, Cathy!"   (Page 15)
Dog pounces on Cathy

Cue 12   The household assemble, **Heathcliff** hangs back   (Page 17)
Sound of a carriage

Cue 13   **Nelly** shows **Heathcliff** the mirror   (Page 19)
Sound of carriage

Cue 14	**Cathy**: "Leave the room, Ellen." *Baby begins to cry*	(Page 24)
Cue 15	**Hindley** can be heard arriving home and swearing *Sound of dogs barking*	(Page 25)
Cue 16	**Cathy**: "Quickly." *Baby cries*	(Page 25)
Cue 17	**Hindley** releases **Nelly** *Baby cries until the end of the scene*	(Page 25)
Cue 18	To open SCENE 10 *Sound of rain*	(Page 26)

ACT II

Cue 19	To open SCENE 4 *Sound of baby crying*	(Page 49)
Cue 20	**Nelly**: "It wasn't the end of the story." *Rain and thunder*	(Page 50)
Cue 21	**Hindley** sits and drinks *Latch rattles*	(Page 50)
Cue 22	**Hindley** runs out *A shot is fired*	(Page 51)
Cue 23	**Joseph** enters *Sound of dogs barking*	(Page 52)
Cue 24	**Lockwood**: "I decided to visit the Heights." *Birds sing*	(Page 62)
Cue 25	**Heathcliff**: " ... was buried I went to the churchyard." *Wind moans, trees creak*	(Page 65)
Cue 26	**Heathcliff**: " Get gone, Mrs Dean!" *Ferocious wind and rain*	(Page 67)
Cue 27	**Nelly** flees *Sound of dogs howling; trees groan and beat against the windows*	(Page 67)
Cue 28	**Nelly** and **Servants** enter and try to close windows *Sound of windows banging*	(Page 67)

Cue 29   **Lockwood** smiles and makes to leave   (Page 69)
              Wind whips up suddenly; rain

Cue 30   **Nelly** appears and watches **Lockwood**   (Page 69)
              Eerie, ghostly sound of children playing and laughing